Iran

Iran

BY BARBARA A. SOMERVILL

Enchantment of the World™
Second Series

Children's Press®

An Imprint of Scholastic Inc.

New York   Toronto   London   Auckland   Sydney
Mexico City   New Delhi   Hong Kong
Danbury, Connecticut

Frontispiece: Shah Mosque, Isfahan

Consultant: Kamran Agahaie, Director of the Center for Middle Eastern Studies, University of
Texas-Austin

Please note: All statistics are as up-to-date as possible at the time of publication.

Book production by The Design Lab

Library of Congress Cataloging-in-Publication Data

Somervill, Barbara A.
 Iran/by Barbara A. Somervill.
    p. cm.—(Enchantment of the world. Second series)
 Includes bibliographical references and index.
 ISBN-13: 978-0-531-25311-3 (lib. bdg.)
 ISBN-10: 0-531-25311-2 (lib. bdg.)
 1. Iran—Juvenile literature. I. Title. II. Series.
 DS254.75.S63 2012
 955—dc23   2011031120

Iran

Contents

Cover photo:
Iranian woman
wearing traditional
nakab mask

Harvesting pistachios

Cheetah

Bargaining at the Bazaar

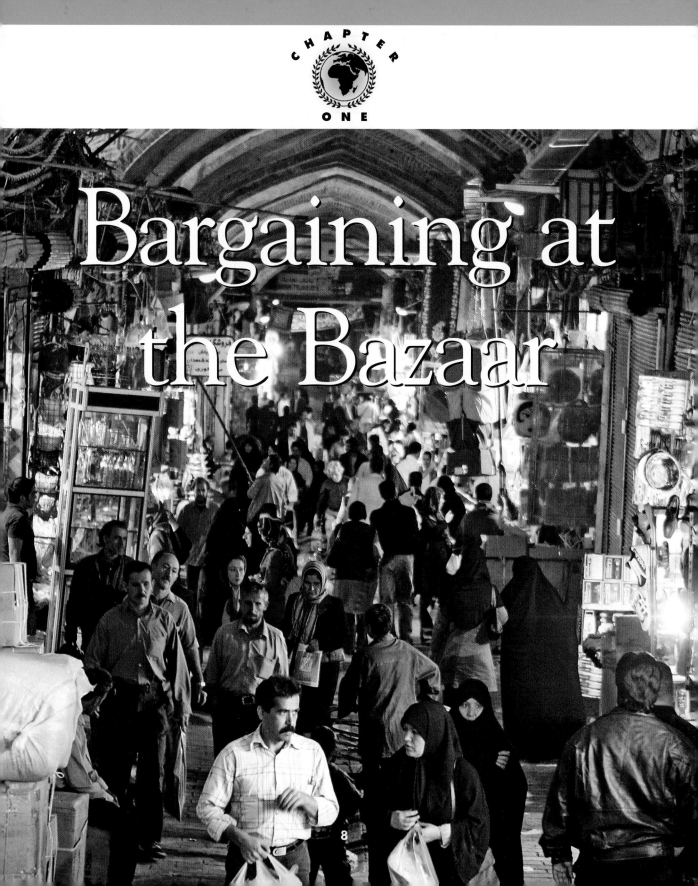

F ARAZ IS UP BEFORE DAWN EACH DAY. AS AN IRANIAN teen, he is expected to work beside his father in the family's shop in the Grand Bazaar of Tehran. The family comes from a long line of goldsmiths who have crafted and sold jewelry, eating utensils, plates, and goblets for nearly a century. One hundred years ago, Faraz would have learned his metalworking skills as an apprentice. Today, he attends a school with other student goldsmiths during the afternoon when business is slow.

The Grand Bazaar of Tehran is a series of permanent, covered shops that are arranged by the items for sale. Goldsmiths line one alley of the bazaar, while the next alley is dedicated to selling copper goods or carpets or shoes. Some corridors in the Grand Bazaar stretch for 6 miles (10 kilometers).

It is just past six o'clock in the evening, and Daria is shopping for a new watch in the Grand Bazaar of Tabriz. She looks through the watches on display and finds one she really wants. Daria knows she can haggle over the price. No one pays what is on the price tag. Bargaining is an honored tradition in Iran's

Opposite: **The shops of the Grand Bazaar of Tehran offer everything form carpets to spices to pots.**

Bargaining at the Bazaar **9**

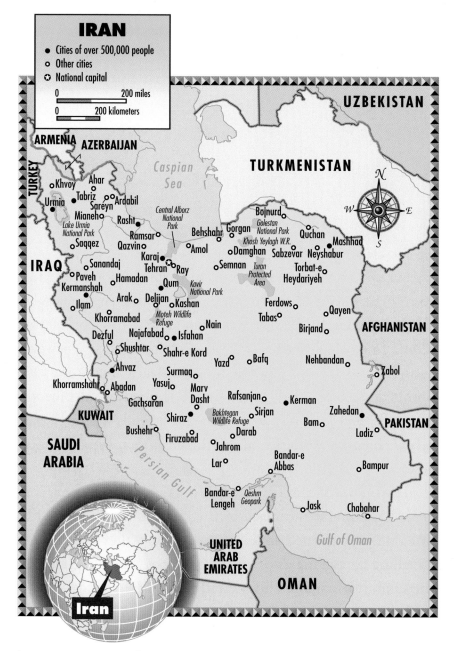

IRAN

- ● Cities of over 500,000 people
- ○ Other cities
- ✪ National capital

0 ————— 200 miles

0 ————— 200 kilometers

UZBEKISTAN

ARMENIA **AZERBAIJAN**

Caspian Sea

TURKMENISTAN

TURKEY

Khvoy   Ahar

Urmia Tabriz Ardabil
        Sareyn
Mianeho
Lake Urmia   Rasht
National Park
        Ramsar
Saqqez Qazvin

Central Alborz National Park

Behshahr Gorgan
Golestan National Park
        Khosh Yeylagh W.R.

Bojnurd

Quchan Mashhad

N

W   **E**

S

Amol

Damghan Sabzevar Neyshabur

IRAQ   Sanandaj

Paveh   Hamadan
Kermanshah

Karaj
Tehran Ray
        Qum

Semnan
Turan Protected Area

Torbat-e Heydariyeh

Ilam
        Arak Delijan Kashan
Khorramabad   *Moteh Wildlife Refuge*
                    Nain

Ferdows

Tabas

Qayen

AFGHANISTAN

Kavir National Park

Dezful Najafabad Isfahan
Shushtar   Shahr-e Kord

Birjand

Ahvaz   Yazd Bafq
        Surmaq

Nehbandan

Zabol

Khorramshahr Abadan Yasuj
                Marv
                Dasht   Rafsanjan
Gachsaran   *Bakhtegan Wildlife Refuge* Sirjan

Kerman
        Bam

Zahedan

PAKISTAN

KUWAIT

SAUDI ARABIA

Shiraz
Bushehr   Firuzabad
                Jahrom
                    Darab

Ladiz

Lar

Bandar-e Abbas

Bampur

Persian Gulf

Bandar-e Lengeh *Qeshm Geopark*

Jask Chabahar

UNITED ARAB EMIRATES

Gulf of Oman

OMAN

Iran

bazaars. Daria makes an offer. The merchant refuses and suggests another price. They go back and forth until buyer and seller are both satisfied with the deal.

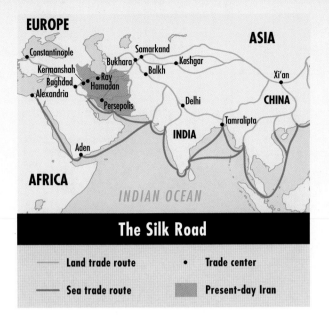

The Silk Road

Land trade route • **Trade center**

Sea trade route ▬ **Present-day Iran**

The Silk Road

The Silk Road was a series of routes that connected China in the Far East to the Roman Empire near the Mediterranean Sea. The routes crossed about 4,000 miles (6,500 km). Silk, spices, and ivory were moved west from China. Silver, gold, and gems traveled east with people from Europe and the Middle East. Several cities in Iran, including Ray, Hamadan, and Kermanshah, were stops along the ancient Silk Road.

The bazaar of Tabriz has existed for more than a thousand years. In its early days, merchants traveled a trade route called the Silk Road in long caravans, with strings of camels laden with silks and spices from the Far East. Bazaars were sometimes set up beside a river, and merchants traded their wares for locally produced goods such as copper kettles or Persian rugs. Cities sprang up in these locations because merchants knew there would be a steady stream of caravans passing through.

Bazaars became the place to go to buy imported goods and sell local fruits, vegetables, and manufactured goods. Travelers slept in large tents or buildings called caravansaries, which also served as warehouses for storing merchandise. As bazaars grew, bathhouses, schools, and mosques were built next to the selling areas. Today, most permanent bazaars have a mosque close by.

Iran has permanent, seasonal, and day bazaars. Permanent bazaars are large marketplaces found in cities such as Isfahan, Shiraz, Tabriz, and Tehran. These bazaars are mazes of corridors and alleyways covered by high, arched ceilings. Many

Most stalls at the bazaar are small, family-run businesses.

of the ceilings are decorated with colored tiles. Permanent bazaars are filled with merchants and craftspeople.

Shahana works at a seasonal bazaar in Panjshanbeh, beside a river that has water for only part of the year. In the spring, her family sells fresh lamb at their stall. The family also sells live chickens, roosters, ducks, and eggs. The family depends on the sales at this seasonal market to provide money for buying clothes, shoes, and household goods. The market also offers fresh fruits, vegetables, and handcrafts such as handwoven cloth and baskets. At seasonal markets, merchants often trade goods with each other, an ancient practice called bartering. Shahana barters two live chickens for a length of dark red cloth shot with gold.

Day bazaars are similar to weekly farmers' markets. They are held in a central location and draw people from throughout a region. Day bazaars are popular in northern Iran and in desert areas. Day bazaars also feature tea sellers, singers, dancers, and musicians.

Bazaars are as central to life in Iran today as they were during the days when travel on the Silk Road was at its peak. Walk through the maze of stalls in a bazaar, and you will experience the color and vigor of Iranian life.

The seafood and meat for sale at bazaars is very fresh.

Deserts and Mountains

14

From the air, the sand dunes of the Dasht-e Lut look like rust-colored ribbons rippling in the breeze. In the distance, rugged mountain peaks rise, capped by glistening white snow. Iran's land is varied and changing. Mountain snows melt, and meltwater pours into a river rushing to the sea. The season changes, and the river water evaporates in the summer heat. In the north, Iran's wetlands teem with life. On the other side of the mountains, barren desert salt flats contain almost no life at all.

Iran shares its southern borders with the Persian Gulf (sometimes called the Arabian Gulf), the Strait of Hormuz, and the Gulf of Oman. To the west lies Iraq and Turkey. Armenia and Azerbaijan are to the northwest, with the Caspian Sea directly north and Turkmenistan on the northeast. The eastern border meets Afghanistan and Pakistan. Iran is the nineteenth-largest country in the world, covering 636,296 square miles (1,648,000 sq km), about four times the size of California.

Opposite: **The Dasht-e Lut is home to ruins of ancient civilizations.**

The Water Cave of `Alisadr

One of the largest water caves in the world, the `Alisadr Cave is a series of underground, natural canals that tourists can travel through on boats. Limestone stalactites, icicle-shaped formations hanging from the cave's roof, are red, purple, green, and blue. The colors come from the minerals mixed in the limestone. The cave was home to early humans, who left behind cave art showing people hunting deer and gazelles with bows and arrows.

Deserts

Most of Iran sits on the Plateau of Iran, a triangular region that is an average of 3,000 to 5,000 feet (900 to 1,500 meters) above sea level. Parts of Pakistan and Afghanistan are also on the Plateau of Iran.

Desert covers much of the plateau. The Dasht-e Kavir stretches across about 240 miles (390 km). The desert is covered with salt crystals rather than sand. Few people live in the Kavir, although there are several oases with freshwater along the southwestern edge of the desert between the cities of Kerman and Qum.

Farther south on the plateau is the Dasht-e Lut, a vast and exceptionally dry desert wasteland that covers an area of about 20,000 square miles (50,000 sq km). The Lut is famed for being the hottest place on Earth, with the temperature once rising to a blistering 159 degrees Fahrenheit (71 degrees Celsius). The desert is a mix of large, shifting sand dunes, sandstone buttes and mesas, and rippling sand patterns caused by the wind. Like

Iran's Geographic Features

Area: 636,296 square miles (1,648,000 sq km)

Highest Elevation: Mount Damavand, 18,806 feet (5,732 m) above sea level

Lowest Elevation: Caspian Sea, 92 feet (28 m) below sea level

Longest Mountain Range: Zagros Mountains, about 930 miles (1,500 km)

Longest River: Karun, 533 miles (858 km)

Largest Lake: Lake Urmia, 1,879 square miles (4,866 sq km)

Largest Desert: Dasht-e Kavir, about 30,000 square miles (78,000 sq km)

Lowest Recorded Temperature: Saqqez, –32.8°F (–36°C)

Highest Recorded Temperature: Dasht-e Lut Desert, 159°F (71°C)

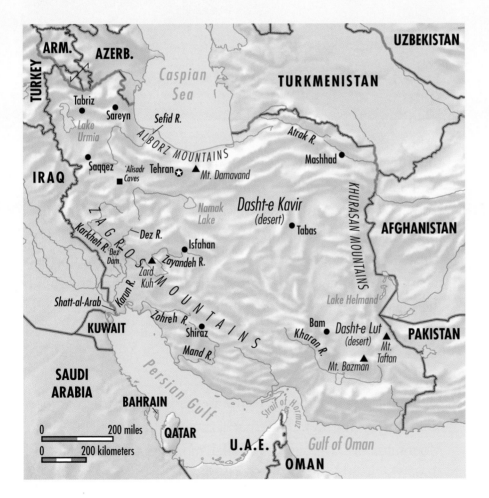

Salt flats are so harsh and dry that almost no plants or animals can live there.

the Kavir, it has some oases with freshwater, but mostly the Lut is a bleak, empty region. Because there are so few plants, wind picks up sand easily, and sandstorms are common. Salt flats and dry lakebeds lie along the eastern boundaries of the Lut. The hottest area of the Dasht-e Lut is Gandom Beryan, which means "toasted wheat" or "burnt wheat." According to legend, the region got its nickname when a load of wheat left in the area was scorched by the sun's heat.

Mountains

Mountains run along most of the western and northern borders of Iran, wrapping around the nation's central deserts. The Alborz Mountains are a group of parallel mountain ranges that curl along the southern shores of the Caspian Sea. The peaks are mostly dormant, or sleeping, volcanoes. Iran's tallest mountain, Mount Damavand, rises to 18,806 feet (5,732 m) above sea level in the middle of the range. In the winter, snow covers the mountain peaks. Many towns and farms lie in the fertile valleys of the Alborz Mountains. Spring sun melts the snow, and the meltwater feeds the rivers and provides fresh water for crops and livestock.

The Zagros Mountains run along the western border of Iran. The mountains end in sheer cliffs at the edge of the Persian Gulf. Rivers that rush through the mountains cut steep ravines and gorges. Some peaks in the Zagros range boast snow year-round. Many of the people living in the Zagros are nomads who raise sheep or goats.

Many small towns and villages are nestled in the Alborz Mountains.

Home of the Gods

In Iranian mythology, Mount Damavand is the home of the gods. In poetry and literature, the fierce three-headed dragon Azi Dahaka is chained within the mountain. The dragon is doomed to live there throughout eternity. The mountain also appears in the legend of Arash, in which Iran and a region called Turan wage a long war over their border. Arash, the hero, was an archer. He shot an arrow as far as he could from the peak of Mount Damavand. The arrow flew throughout the morning and landed by the banks of the Oxus River. For centuries, the Oxus was considered the symbolic border between Iran and Turan.

Bodies of Water

Iran's largest bodies of water are the Caspian Sea in the north and the Persian Gulf and Gulf of Oman in the south. Although the Caspian is called a sea, it is technically a large saltwater lake that is fed from the north by the Volga, Ural, and Terek Rivers. Iran's Caspian coastline is dotted with sandy beaches, natural wetlands, and summer resorts.

The Persian Gulf and the Gulf of Oman provide shipping routes in southern Iran. The Iranian shoreline along the Persian Gulf is mountainous, with rugged cliffs, narrow beaches, and scattered ports.

Iran has few lakes, and most are small. Many of the smallest lakes dried up during a serious drought that affected Iran from 1998 to 2001. In 1900, Lake Helmand, a lake along the Afghanistan border, measured just under 58,000 square miles (150,000 sq km). During the twentieth century, the lake shrank to 12,400 square miles (32,000 sq km). When the drought struck, Lake Helmand dried up almost completely.

The largest lake totally within Iran is Lake Urmia, located in the northwest. The lake changes size with the seasons, but at its largest measures about 1,879 square miles (4,866 sq km). Lake Urmia has extensive salt marshes on the eastern and southern shores. Algae in the very salty water feed the limited fish and crustaceans. Waterbirds, such as flamingos and ducks, feed on brine shrimp that live in the lake.

Many of Iran's rivers are dry in the late summer and autumn and are rushing torrents when mountain snows melt

Large numbers of flamingos flock to Lake Urmia when it is time for them to mate.

in the spring. Iran's largest river is the Karun, which runs 533 miles (858 km) from the Zagros Mountains to the Persian Gulf. Although the Karun is a navigable river—the lone one in Iran—only small ships and boats can travel on it. The Karkheh and Dez Rivers run from the Zagros to the south. The Sefid Rud and Atrak drain into the Caspian in the north.

Sleeping Giants, Shaking Earth

Eight active or semiactive volcanoes lie in the Alborz Mountains. Damavand, the largest volcano, is cone-shaped with a small crater at the top. Although Damavand has been dormant, or sleeping, for more than seven thousand years, it has the potential to erupt. Fumaroles, openings that emit gases and steam, are active at Damavand's peak. Fumaroles are also active on Taftan and Bazman.

The Earthquake at Bam

On December 26, 2003, Bam, Iran, suffered a deadly earthquake that measured 6.6 on the Richter scale, which measures an earthquake's power. The quake destroyed 85 percent of the city's buildings. More than half of the 115,000 residents were left homeless, and more than 15,000 were killed. Once a crossroads for the silk and cotton trade routes, Bam is an excellent example of a fortified medieval town built using mud layers. But this ancient building technique left the city vulnerable to the earthquake that destroyed so much of it.

Sleeping volcanoes don't present much danger to Iranians, but major faults, which are cracks in Earth's crust, do. Iran's fault lines run through the Alborz and the Zagros ranges. Iran suffers frequent earthquakes because it lies at the meeting place of two of the gigantic tectonic plates that make up Earth's outer layer. As these plates slowly slide against each other, earthquakes occur.

Nearly every day, Iran has some type of earthquake. Most are minor and are only detected by scientific instruments. In the past one hundred years, however, Iran has suffered a dozen serious earthquakes. In the twentieth century, more than 126,000 Iranians died from earthquakes.

Hot and Dry, Cold and Wet

Iran's climate includes places where there is no rainfall from one year to the next, as well as areas that are drenched with rain. It ranges from bitter cold winters in the Zagros Mountains to the hottest spot on Earth in the Dasht-e Lut. Iran's many climates range from subtropical to sub-Arctic. Most of Iran's climate is best described as harsh.

Iran's overall average precipitation is about 11 inches (28 centimeters). Most of that rain falls in the winter and spring. Because the rainfall is heavy over a short period, the soil cannot absorb the water, and flash floods race down dry riverbeds.

Some of Iran's desert regions have no measurable rainfall, and in some places, it is so hot and dry that rain evaporates before reaching the ground. This unusual occurrence is called virga. Typically, less than 12 inches (30 cm) of rain falls on

Mount Tochal is one of the many places Iranians can enjoy snow during the winter.

Iran's steppe, or grasslands region, each year. The steppe is covered with a sparse mix of low shrubs and scruffy grass tufts.

The Caspian coast is hot and wet during the summer, receiving about 80 inches (200 cm) of rainfall. This rain supports wetlands and dense forests on the northern slopes of the Alborz Mountains. The region also has many fields of rice and some mucky swamps.

Temperatures in Iran vary according to the region. The deserts are hot throughout the year, with summer daytime temperatures exceeding 100°F (38°C). Temperatures drop by as much as 40°F (22°C) at night in the desert. In the winter, frost forms in some parts of the Dasht-e Kavir. The mountain regions have cold winters, with plenty of snow for skiing and sledding.

Iran has two distinctive winds—so distinctive that they have names. The *shamal* blows from February to October in a northwesterly direction. During the height of the summer, the "120-day wind," or *levar*, whips in the southeast. This wind

From 1998 to 2001, Iran suffered its worst drought in thirty years. The drought affected more than sixty million people, as lakes and rivers dried up and disappeared. Nearly three million tons of wheat withered in the fields. Seventy percent of the nation's water supply was disrupted, and the lack of water drove millions of people from rural villages into cities that were unprepared for the increased population. City residents endured power cuts, as hydroelectric plants that depend on rushing water to run were unable to produce enough electricity to meet demands. When the rains finally came, flash floods washed away soil from empty fields and sent people wading across flooded rivers to seek drier, safer land.

races across the land at speeds up to 100 miles (160 km) per hour, picking up sand and dust. The levar usually begins in June and lasts until September.

Conservation

Iran's major cities suffer from poor air quality. The heavy use of old and poorly maintained cars is responsible for more than three-fourths of the air pollution in Tehran, Isfahan, and Mashhad. The cities are also industrial centers, and factories contribute to the smog that blankets these cities. The government is trying to reduce air pollution by encouraging taxis and buses to convert from gasoline engines to engines that run on compressed natural gas. Natural gas produces much less air pollution than regular gasoline.

A Look at Iran's Cities

Tehran, Iran's capital and largest city, is home to about 8,430,000. With a population of 2,965,000, Mashhad is Iran's second-largest city. It is located in northeastern Iran near the border with Afghanistan. Mashhad is the country's holiest city, site of the Haram-e Razavi, a shrine to Imam Reza, one of Iran's holiest religious leaders. The outer courtyards of the site are open to all, but the inner sanctuaries are holy shrines and open only to Muslims. The city also boasts several museums, including a stamp museum, a Persian carpet museum, and a museum dedicated to calligraphy, or ornate handwriting.

Shiraz (below), known as the House of Learning and the City of Roses, has a population of 1,750,000. Shiraz has an active bazaar, shopping centers, colorful gardens, parks, and stunningly beautiful mosques. The city is home to one of Iran's oldest mosques, the

Martyrs' Mosque, and one of the nation's most beautiful mosques, the Nasir al-Molk Mosque.

The 1,630,000 citizens of Isfahan (above) are proud of their city, often considered the jewel of Iran. The city's mosques have beautifully patterned blue tile work. The Jameh Mosque is now a museum rather than a house of worship, and visitors can trace the heritage of Islamic architecture as they move from one hall to the next. The city also houses two magnificent palaces, the Ali Qapu Palace and the Chehel Sotun Palace. Both palaces have fine examples of Iranian art. Ali Qapu has beautiful carved and inlaid woodwork, and Chehel Sotun has magnificent wall murals.

Wetland conservation is another important environmental issue in Iran. Many wetland areas dried up during the drought of 1998 to 2001. Iranian wetlands have been drained to provide water for human use and irrigation. Other wetland areas have been destroyed by road construction, shrimp and fish farming, or farmland development. The situation involving wetlands is difficult. Iran's people need fresh water and food, and it is hard to value wetlands over people in need.

In the south, the Persian Gulf and Gulf of Oman suffer from heavy pollution caused by oil tankers, shipping, and naval vessels. Iran's main rivers also empty industrial pollution and raw sewage into these waters. The Persian Gulf is particularly delicate because it is shallow and mostly enclosed by land, with only a narrow outlet. Much of the pollution is caught in the gulf and cannot be washed away by ocean tides. The Iranian government is trying to control pollution in their seas, but the problems are many and solutions are few.

Moving Water

A land that has little water needs to find the best ways to use what fresh water it has. Ancient Iranians created a network of underground canals called *qanats*. There are nearly fifty thousand qanats that have provided water for irrigation for centuries. A qanat lets water move long distances with little loss from evaporation. Because water is such a problem in Iran, engineers who specialize in water use think that increased use of qanats will ease serious water shortages caused by droughts.

Deserts and Mountains **27**

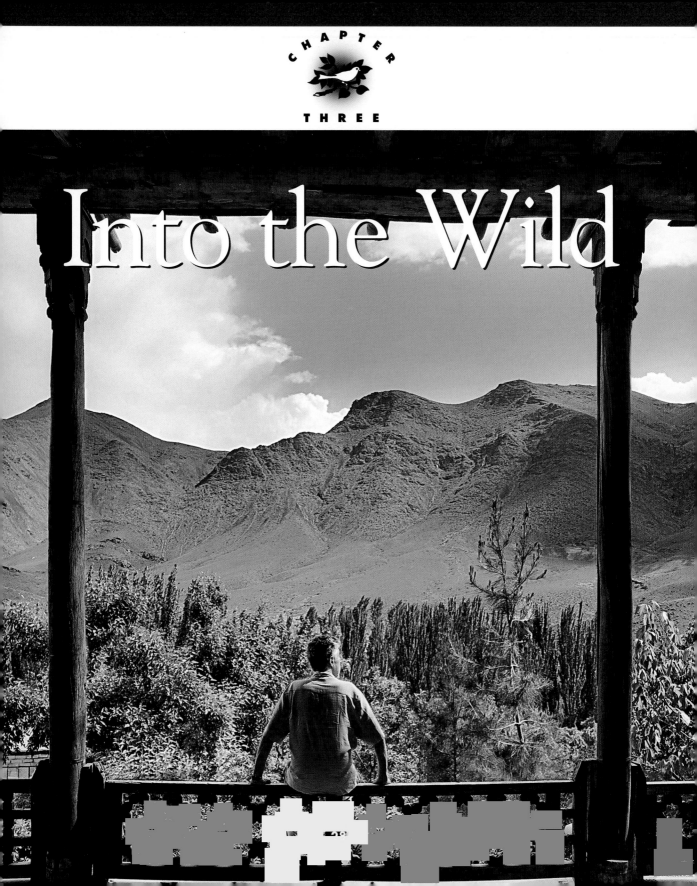

Into the Wild

IRAN'S LANDSCAPE RANGES FROM DENSE FORESTS TO marshy wetlands to dry-as-a-bone deserts. Forests and wetlands abound with life, and even some desert areas support their share of palms, tamarisks, snakes, and rodents.

About one-tenth of Iran is covered with forests. Most forests are found on the northern slopes of the Alborz Mountains and in the Zagros Mountains. The forests have a mix of trees that provide a burst of green in spring and summer, and touches of red and gold in the autumn. Common trees include oak, ash, elm, and beech. Varieties of juniper keep the woods green throughout the year.

In the Zagros Mountains, oak is the most common tree, but the region also has wild walnut, pear, and pistachio trees. Juniper and pistachio also grow well on dry plateaus. At lower elevations, springtime acacia explodes with tiny golden blooms.

Desert oases support a surprising number of trees and shrubs. Tamarisk, or salt cedar, has small leaves and very thin branches. It looks delicate and fernlike, with pale pink flowers on the ends of each branch. Mulberry, plum, and acacia trees

Opposite: **A man looks out over the landscape near Shiraz, in southwestern Iran.**

also grow in oasis areas as do date palms, a favorite among travelers. In the hotter desert regions of Iran, date palms provide welcome shade and fronds heavy with sweet, juicy dates.

Spring wildflowers splash color in mountain meadows and hillsides. Yellow buttercups, red geraniums, and rich pink wild tulips stand in contrast to the greenery. Plum, barberry, and delicate orchids grow wild in the countryside.

In the south, mangroves—unusual trees that grow in salt water—stretch their knobby-kneed roots along the Iranian

Wildflowers bloom during Iran's pleasant spring.

coast. Called *hara* in Iran, mangroves have a tangle of roots that provide important habitats for young fish, crustaceans, and wading birds. The hara tree has bright green leaves and yellow flowers, and bears a sweet fruit that tastes like almonds.

Wild Animals

An abundance of wild fruits and nuts provide native plant-eating animals with food. Iran is home to many large mammals, including ibex, red deer, roe deer, wild sheep, and gazelles. Smaller mammals such as rabbits, hares, and ground squirrels thrive on forest nuts and berries. In some parts of the desert, small herds of wild asses browse on saltbush and tamarisk. Wild asses once numbered in the thousands, but poaching and habitat loss have reduced their numbers to fewer than four hundred.

These plant-eating animals are preyed on by powerful predators. The largest are Asiatic cheetahs, leopards, wolves, and jackals. Cheetahs and leopards hunt as individuals. Cheetahs are daytime hunters, relying on their speed to bring

The Asiatic Cheetah

Cheetahs in general are an endangered species, but the Asiatic cheetah of Iran is exceptionally rare. In east-central Iran, the cats live solitary lives in treeless plains, tall grasses, and scrub bushes. They hunt gazelles, goats, oryx, and lynx. The habitat of these speedy hunters is disappearing, and many young die before they are three months old. Iran's government has created a cheetah preservation plan that establishes designated cheetah zones. It is believed that only seventy to one hundred Asiatic cheetahs presently survive in Iran.

down gazelles, wild sheep, or oryx. Persian leopards are light tan with dark splotches in their fur. There are between 550 and 850 Persian leopards in Iran, living mainly in the Alborz and Zagros Mountains and feeding on goats, deer, gazelles, urials (wild sheep), and wild boars. Wolves and jackals are related to dogs and hunt in packs or pairs. Jackals are scavengers, meaning that they are happy to feed on the remains of an animal killed by a larger predator, but they also hunt for themselves. Foxes and Eurasian lynx hunt the rodents that live in mountains and foothills.

Iran has 527 species of birds that live full- or part-time in the country. Pelicans, ibis, spoonbills, and storks nest in wetland areas. The seacoast plays host to gulls, terns, and sandpipers. Iranians have a history of raising falcons and hawks for hunting. In the wild, eagles and ospreys snatch fish from rivers and lakes. At night, owls swoop through the darkness,

plucking squirrels and mice from the forest floor. Long-legged flamingos, geese, and ducks enjoy the brine shrimp that thrive in the waters of Lake Urmia.

Maynard's longnose sand snake can be found in Iran's desert regions.

Amphibians and reptiles fare well in Iran's foothills and lower mountain regions. Toads, frogs, and turtles settle in the muck around small ponds and marshes. Iran has sixty snake species, including venomous vipers and cat snakes. Rat snakes

Endangered Species

Iran has a number of endangered species that the nation hopes to preserve. The government has set aside preserves and protected areas in which hunting and fishing are either limited or totally banned. Among the species Iran's conservationists worry most about are Caspian seals, Asiatic black bears, Asiatic wild asses, Asiatic cheetahs, wild goats, and urials.

and sand boas help control the rodent populations in the dry plateau and semiarid desert regions.

Because Iran has lakes and rivers that are wet only during the winter and spring, freshwater fish are limited to a few rivers. One species regularly fished from Alborz and Zagros streams is mountain trout. Other native species include varieties of bream, sturgeon, shad, carp, loach, and barbel. Several species of sturgeon are fished in the Caspian Sea. People harvest the sturgeon eggs and sell them as an expensive food called caviar.

More than seven hundred species of fish and crustaceans live in the Persian Gulf and the Gulf of Oman. Most of the fish live around coral reefs, which are under constant threat. Pollution and tourists diving near and damaging reefs have destroyed some reefs, and the government is working to control further destruction of coral reef habitats.

Many unusual fish species, such as the red lionfish, live near the Gulf of Oman's coral reefs.

Among the marvelous creatures living in the Persian Gulf is the dugong, a marine mammal known as the sea cow. Dugongs graze on sea grass along the seafloor. Hawksbill sea turtles, an endangered species, lay their eggs on Iranian island beaches in the gulf.

Hawksbill sea turtles depend on Iran's beaches as nesting areas.

Watch Out!

The Gulf of Oman has some dangerous species that humans need to watch out for. Fire coral is a green, branched coral that is highly toxic. Just touching the surface causes a blistery rash. The Portuguese man-of-war (left) has a bluish-purple sac, which floats on the water, and thick tentacles that are capable of painful stings. Three jellyfish—the little mauve jellyfish, the cone-shaped jellyfish, and the bell-shaped jellyfish—pack a real wallop. The bell-shaped jelly can cause cramps, vomiting, and paralysis in anyone it stings. Equally venomous are the spotfin lionfish and the devil scorpion fish. A tiny prick from either of these critters may cause heart problems, pain, paralysis, and convulsions.

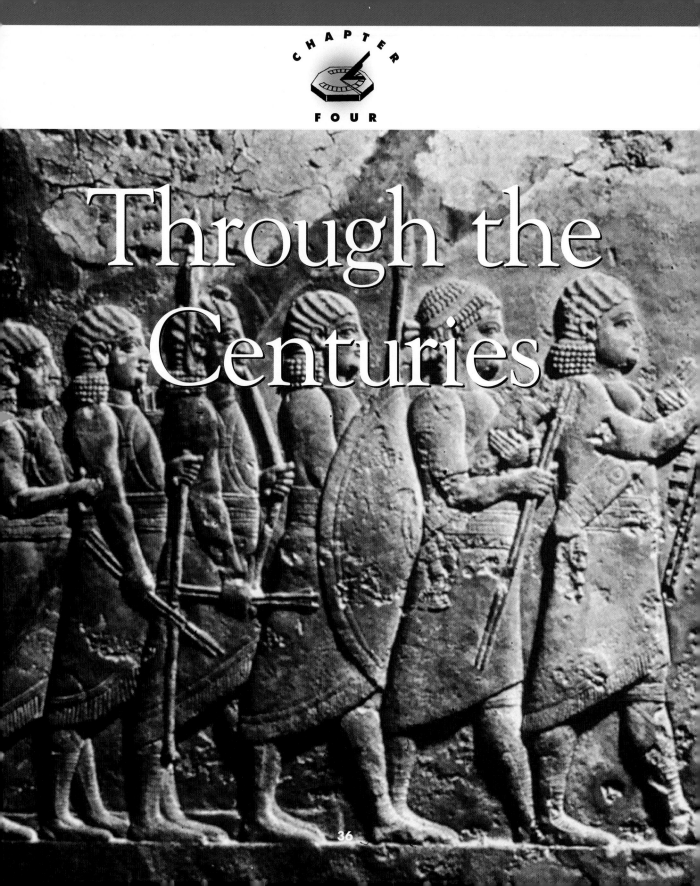

Through the Centuries

THE EARLIEST HUMANS IN IRAN WERE HUNTER-GATHERERS who lived in family groups known as clans. The men hunted big game. The women gathered nuts and berries. The clans lived in caves in the Zagros Mountains.

Opposite: **Ancient Iranians hunted using spears and bows.**

Scientists and historians believe humans have lived on the Iranian plateau for one hundred thousand years. They learn about early people from bones, flint knives, and cave paintings. By studying human bones, scientists can figure out to what age people lived, how long ago they lived, what diseases they suffered from, and what they ate. Flint knives indicate that people made and used tools, and cave paintings depict their hunts. The earliest Iranians hunted deer and caught fish using flint spearheads.

The hunter-gatherer lifestyle was nomadic. Clans traveled from one camp to the next, following game animals. That lifestyle existed on the Iranian plateau until about 10,000 BCE, when large game had been overhunted, and people settled in small villages. They built huts, raised wheat and barley, and began to tame wild animals for use as farm animals. By 6000 BCE, farming villages were common throughout the plateau.

The Elamites were the first organized culture in Iran. They lived in the lowlands of the southwest. Established about five thousand years ago, the Elamite kingdom had its capital at Susa. Elam had a government that arranged trading with its neighbors. Over the centuries, the kingdom developed close contact with Sumer, Babylonia, and Assyria through trade and war. The Elamite kingdom ended when King Khumma-Khaldash III died in 644 BCE.

The Medes were six tribes that formed a loose group in the northwestern area of Iran. Fierce warriors, the Medes raised horses, built castles, and established fortresses against invaders. Their capital city was Ecbatana, currently known as Hamadan. Few buildings from the early days of Ecbatana are left, but archaeologists have been digging in the area and recovering some ancient remains.

The Medes occupied the northern region of present-day Iran; people known as Persians lived in Pars to the south. In

Zarathustra

Zarathustra (ca. 628–ca. 551 BCE) was a prophet and religious leader of ancient Iran. He was also known by the Greek version of his name, Zoroaster. Zarathustra taught that Ahura Mazda was the only god worthy of prayer. Zarathustra's supporters followed the Avesta, which are scriptures, and sang hymns called *gathas*, some of which may have been written by Zarathustra himself. Today, there are between 145,000 and 210,000 Zoroastrians, mostly in Iran, Pakistan, and India, where they are called Parsis.

Cyrus the Great is also known as Cyrus the Elder.

559 BCE, troops led by the Persian king Cyrus II, also known as Cyrus the Great, overran the Medes. Cyrus united the Persians and the Medes into the Achaemenian Empire.

The Achaemenian Empire

Cyrus the Great ruled from 559 to 529 BCE. The empire expanded under Cyrus as he conquered neighboring cultures, such as Drangiana, Arachosia, Margiana, and Bactria. Cyrus led his army into Babylon and Egypt, and was known for his kindness and generosity toward the people he conquered.

Cyrus developed the first known charter of human rights, which declared equality among people of different races, languages, and religious beliefs. His political ideas were so

The Empire of Babylon

Cyrus's greatest feat was conquering the powerful Babylonian civilization in 539 BCE. At the time, Babylon was the center of learning and science. It was also a warring nation that made slaves of its captives. When Cyrus defeated Babylon, he freed the forty thousand Jewish slaves and liberated many other people oppressed by the Babylonians.

admired that many of Iran's future emperors followed Cyrus's ideas. A copy of the Cyrus Cylinder, the clay tablet that recorded his human rights policies, is on display in the United Nations Building in New York City.

Archaeologists discovered the Cyrus Cylinder in 1879.

The Achaemenian rulers included some of Iran's greatest ancient military and political leaders. Darius I, who came to power in 522 BCE, gained control of the Punjab region of India and an area extending as far west as the Danube River in Europe. He began building Persepolis, the capital city. With Darius, Iran began two hundred years of prosperity. His son Xerxes succeeded him and reigned from 486 to 465 BCE.

The empire was so vast that it was hard to control. When the Egyptians and Babylonians rebelled, Xerxes sent in his army. In 480 BCE, Xerxes defeated the Greek forces under King Leonidas. Persian troops occupied Athens and burned the Parthenon, the Greek temple of Athena. The Greek navy then faced the Persian ships off Salamis and destroyed Xerxes's navy.

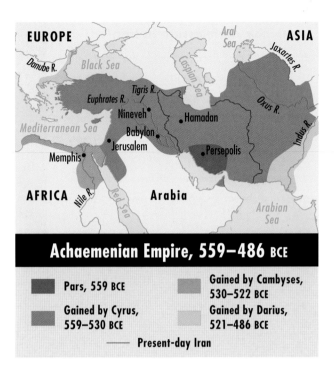

Achaemenian Empire, 559–486 BCE

Pars, 559 BCE

Gained by Cyrus, 559–530 BCE

Gained by Cambyses, 530–522 BCE

Gained by Darius, 521–486 BCE

—— Present-day Iran

The Achaemenian Empire ended when it was invaded by Alexander the Great in 332 BCE. Alexander's troops took over Persepolis and destroyed the city. When Alexander the Great died in 323 BCE, he left no instructions about who should lead in his place. Alexander's generals divided up his empire, and Seleucus took over the Achaemenian lands.

The Seleucid Empire stretched from Turkey to India. This extensive land included trade routes along the Silk Road. Iran was at the center of this trade, and Iranian cities flourished as

Greek Architecture in Iran

At the end of the Seleucid reign, the Parthians swarmed into Iran from the northeast and took over. They brought with them Greek culture and the artistry of Greek architecture. The Parthians built open, three-walled buildings that allowed air to flow easily. These open courtyards, called *iwans*, became a significant part of Iranian architecture and are found in palaces, mosques, and shrines throughout present-day Iran.

travelers passed through. Iranians sold carpets, copper tools, grape seeds, cotton fabric, horses, and camels. These items were taken both east to China and west to Europe.

The Sasanians

By 224 CE, the Sasanians had risen to power. During Sasanian rule, Zoroastrianism became the official religion of the land. The various parts of the Avesta were brought together and compiled into one prayer book.

The Sasanians established a central government under a king. All provincial officials reported to the king, and the government built roads and city buildings. The language of the Sasanians was Pahlavi, the language in which most Zoroastrian works were written. Learning was important, and scholars spent time translating literature of the Far East and Europe into Pahlavi.

Art and architecture flourished during Sasanian times. Kings built large, fancy palaces, such as those found in

Ctesiphon, the Sasanian capital. Artists carved rock sculptures into cliffs at sites such as Bishapur.

Arabs and the Rise of Islam

The Prophet Muhammad, who first spread the word of Islam, died in 632 CE. After this, the religion spread rapidly throughout the Middle East. In 651, Arabs swept into the Sasanian Empire, bringing Islamic beliefs with them. Over several centuries, Muslims became the majority in Iran, although large non-Muslim communities remained.

Muslims allowed citizens the freedom to choose their own religion. Jews and Christians had a lower status than Muslims, but they were not systematically persecuted for what they believed. Muslims brought many new ideas to Iran. Arabic writing and numbers replaced the more difficult Pahlavi written language.

Mosques appeared throughout the Middle East as Islam spread.

The Prophet Muhammad

The name Muhammad means "highly praised," and it was a fitting name for the Prophet Muhammad. Muhammad was born in Mecca, in western Arabia, around 570. He believed that God, called Allah in Arabic, sent him a series of revelations. He had a personal vision of the angel Gabriel telling him of Allah's path to a holy life. The revelations were later compiled into the Qur'an. In 619, Muhammad faced a difficult period in his life. He had lost both his wife, Khadijah, and the chief of his clan, Abu Talib, who was his primary protector. Muhammad moved to Medina, another city in Arabia, where many people followed his teachings. More and more people converted to Islam, and by 651, Islam had spread to the Iranian plateau.

The Seljuq Dynasty

After Muslims came to power in the region, Turkic-speaking tribes of central Asia began to move into northern Iran. They were nomadic warriors who were often hired for military purposes. In 1020, the ruler of Khwarizm (Turkmenistan) hired the Seljuqs. The Seljuqs quickly decided that following orders was not as profitable as giving orders. The Seljuqs took over and spread their rule across Iran.

The Seljuq rulers followed the Sunni sect of Islam. They built mosques in cities such as Hamadan, Kerman, and Isfahan. The Seljuqs supported arts, mainly pottery, jewelry making, and carpet making. Although they were warriors, the Seljuqs wanted peace.

The Mongol Invasion

In 1220, Genghis Khan, the leader of Mongolia, a region in east-central Asia, invaded Iran. While all invasions were brutal during this time, the Mongol invasion was unusual in that it disrupted some government and economic systems that previous invaders had left in place. The Mongol army burned villages and crops and ruined many underground irrigation systems that allowed the Iranians to water their crops.

In 1295, Ghazan, a Mongol leader of Iran, converted to Islam. He worked to improve government, expand agriculture, and increase trade in Iran. Travel across the Silk Road increased, since by this time the Mongol Empire controlled the entire route from China to Turkey and could ensure some safety for traveling merchants.

By the mid-1300s, Iran had a new Mongol ruler, Timur, also known as Tamerlane. Timur struck terror in the hearts of those he conquered. He destroyed cities, enslaved conquered people, and killed thousands. He had little interest in trade but conquered cultures to steal their wealth.

A Great Poet

Omar Khayyám (ca. 1048–ca. 1132 CE) was an Iranian astronomer and mathematician, but he is best remembered in the English-speaking world as the poet who wrote the *The Rubáiyát of Omar Khayyám*. This long poem consists of 101 four-line stanzas, which present Khayyám's feelings about life, death, love, and religion.

Through the Centuries **45**

Timur became the ruler of much of central Asia, conquering India, Syria, Turkey, and Iran. After his death in 1405, his empire fell apart as his sons and grandsons bickered over who would become the next leader.

The Safavids

In 1501, a man named Ismail led an army that would eventually take over all of Iran, Azerbaijan, part of Armenia, and most of Afghanistan. He became Shah (king) Ismail I of Iran at age fifteen. Ismail founded the Safavid Empire.

In 1587, Shah Abbas, the greatest Safavid leader, moved the capital to Isfahan, which became a model city of its time. Abbas established diplomatic links with major European nations and came to be called Abbas the Great.

Abbas the Great ruled Iran until 1629.

The Qajar Dynasty

In 1779, the Qajar dynasty took control of Iran. The Qajars were Turkmen from the area currently known as Turkmenistan. Aga Mohammed Khan, the first Qajar leader, moved the capital to Tehran in 1795.

Over the next one hundred years, Iran became a pawn in the worldwide power game. Great Britain traded with Iran, both directly and through its colonies of Australia, India, Egypt, and Malaysia. Russia was interested in Iran because

Iran had ports on the Persian Gulf and the Gulf of Oman. Russia's ports froze during the winter, and a warm-water port would help with international trade in India and the Far East. Great Britain wanted to prevent Russia from gaining too much influence in Iran. Iran's leaders began relying on British money to help pay the nation's bills.

Modernizing Iran

In the late 1800s, Nasser al-Din Shah undertook a scheme to modernize Iran. He collected art, built museums and palaces, and lived lavishly. To bring in more money, Nasser al-Din sold the rights to start banks, mine natural resources, build railroads, and process Iran's tobacco to Great Britain. But the shah kept the money for himself. As his wealth increased, Iran's people continued to struggle.

In 1906, Iranian leaders forced the next shah, Muzaffar al-Din, to form the Majles, a group of elected lawmakers. A constitution was written, limiting the shah's power. This period was called the Constitutional Revolution.

Oil was discovered in Iran in 1908. The British funded oil exploration, wells, and refineries. They formed the Anglo-Persian Oil Company, later called the Anglo-Iranian Oil Company. The oil industry made huge profits, but most of the money went to British interests.

The Last Shahs

In 1921, Reza Pahlavi, a clever, popular military officer, organized the overthrow of the Qajar shah. At first, Pahlavi supported a prime minister, Ahmad Shah, as Iran's government head. By 1925, he had replaced Ahmad Shah, and the Majles officially elected Pahlavi to be shah. He became known as Reza Shah Pahlavi.

Reza Shah favored Western ways over traditional Iranian ways. Courts were no longer under the control of religious leaders. Women did not wear veils, as they were previously supposed to do. For the first time, women were allowed to divorce their husbands. Both boys and girls attended school, and women were allowed to go to college.

Reza Shah brought great changes to Iran.

In the 1930s, Reza Shah, hoping to control the influence of the British and Russians on Iran's economy, turned to a new trading partner, Germany. In 1941, in the midst of World War II, the British and the Russians were fighting Germany, and they invaded Iran because there were so many Germans there. British and Russian forces removed Reza Shah from power, and his son Mohammad Reza Shah Pahlavi took the throne.

After World War II, Iranians began the First Development Plan (1948–1955), which called for major changes in agriculture and industry. The government needed money to pay for the plan and intended to use profits from oil sales. The main oil company at the

time was the Anglo-Iranian Oil Company (AIOC). Most of its profits still went to Great Britain.

In 1951, the Majles negotiated with the AIOC over equal profit sharing. When the Majles succeeded in increasing their share of the money, British oil technicians left the country. With no skilled Iranian technicians, oil production came to a standstill. Great Britain refused to buy Iranian oil and froze Iranian money in British banks.

In Iran, Prime Minister Mohammad Mosaddeq and Reza Shah had opposite views about the oil crisis. Mosaddeq led

Mohammad Reza Shah Pahlavi (on throne) ruled Iran from 1941 until 1979.

Mohammad Mosaddeq was popular among the people of Iran.

protesters against the shah's forces. Although the shah's army defeated the protesters, hundreds of people were injured, many were arrested, and several were executed during the rebellion.

In the 1960s, Islamic leaders protested the shah's ties to Western nations. The leader of these protests was Ayatollah Ruhollah Khomeini. To stop the protests, in 1963 the shah had Khomeini put in prison and later exiled from Iran.

The Islamic Revolution

By the late 1970s, Iran was a country steeped in protests. On the surface, Iran's economy was expanding, oil sales were high, and the country was becoming more modern.

In 1978, a Tehran newspaper made negative remarks about Ayatollah Khomeini, who was then living in Paris, France. Students from one of Tehran's Islamic schools flocked to the streets in protest. The shah was suffering from cancer and unable to deal with a rebellion. Government forces tried to end the demonstrations, but the protests only grew. Khomeini kept in close contact with protest leaders and spurred on the rebellion. By January 1979, it was clear that the shah was losing power, and he left Iran. Khomeini arrived in Iran on February 1, 1979, and took control.

Khomeini and his followers declared Iran an Islamic republic. They placed Islamic clerics in key roles in the government and established the Assembly of Experts to write a new constitution. Under the new government, Islamic law was incorporated into the law of the land. Women were expected to cover their heads and bodies when in public. Although people were allowed to vote on their government leaders, only candidates approved by Shi'i religious leaders could run for office.

From 1980 to 1988, Iran and its neighbor Iraq fought a war over the border in southwestern Iran. Iraq invaded the region, which is one of Iran's main oil-producing areas. The war was bloody. More than half a million Iranians had died by the time the Iran-Iraq War ended in August 1988.

Iran-Iraq War, 1980–1988

- Occupied by Iraq, 1980–1982
- Occupied by Iran, 1985–1988
- Oil field
- Present-day borders

Khomeini died in 1989 and was replaced by Ayatollah Sayyed Ali Khamenei, who is the current supreme leader. That same year, a new constitution was written, which called for the election of a president. The first president was Akbar Hashemi Rafsanjani, who served from 1989 to 1997. Khamenei and Rafsanjani took a more moderate approach to governing. Many laws put in place under Khomeini were no longer enforced as strictly.

Ayatollah Mohammad Khatami was elected to the presidency in 1997. Khatami wanted to improve the lives of Iranians by giving

Before becoming president, Hashemi Rafsanjani played a major role in ending the Iran-Iraq War.

Fighting for Rights

In 2003, Shirin Ebadi (1947–) became the first Iranian to be awarded the Nobel Peace Prize. She was chosen because of her open and aggressive fight for human rights and democracy in Iran. A lawyer by profession, Ebadi regularly took on cases that other Iranian lawyers avoided. She clashed with conservative leaders who attacked Iranians fighting for reform. Ebadi had once served as a judge, but she was forced to resign in 1979, because women could no longer be judges in the Islamic republic. Despite the laws controlling women in Iran, Ebadi continues to fight for women's rights and greater freedom for all Iranians.

them more personal freedoms. He also wanted to establish friendly relationships with several Western nations. Under Iran's government organization, the president is not as powerful as the supreme leader. Khatami came up against strong opposition from the supreme leader and other powerful conservatives. He was unable to fulfill many of his political promises.

In 2005, Mahmoud Ahmadinejad, a conservative former mayor of Tehran, became president. Iran by this time was working on a nuclear program to provide energy to the nation. Many people in the West feared that the nuclear fuel Iran could produce would instead be used in nuclear weapons. Only time will tell whether Iran is actually producing nuclear weapons.

The First
Islamic Republic

THE 1979 ISLAMIC REVOLUTION CHANGED HOW IRAN'S government and politics worked. The shah was ousted, and along with him went many of the laws and policies that governed Iranians. In came the Ayatollah Ruhollah Khomeini as supreme leader, a position that was created by the country's new constitution.

The constitution established the first Islamic republic, a government in which Islamic clerics, or religious leaders, play a role in supervising the three branches of government—executive, legislative, and judiciary. A high-ranking cleric heads both the government and the Islamic groups overseeing the government.

Opposite: **A group of religious leaders called the Assembly of Experts chooses the supreme leader.**

Overseeing the Government

Iran has several religious groups that supervise the workings of the government. These committees include the Assembly of Experts, the Guardian Council, and the Supreme Defense Council.

The Assembly of Experts was first established by Ayatollah Khomeini to develop Iran's 1979 constitution. The assembly

Ruhollah Khomeini

The Grand Ayatollah Ruhollah Khomeini (1902–1989), an Islamic scholar, was revered as a leading cleric in Shi'i Islam. Khomeini was put in prison for speaking out against Mohammad Reza Shah Pahlavi. He fled to Iraq and then moved to Paris, France, where he stayed in touch with Iran's politically active student groups. In 1979, Khomeini returned to Iran following the overthrow of the shah's government. Khomeini was the first supreme leader of the newly formed Islamic Republic of Iran.

consists of eighty-six religious leaders who are elected by Iran's citizens. The Assembly of Experts appoints the supreme leader and monitors his performance as a government head and primary religious leader. Elections to the assembly are held every eight years.

The Guardian Council consists of six Islamic scholars who are appointed by the supreme leader and six justices who are chosen by members of Iran's judiciary branch. Since most justices are Islamic legal scholars, the six justices are likely to be clerics as well.

The Guardian Council reviews all candidates for president and the legislature, and can bar a candidate from running for election. The council reviews bills passed in the legislature and can veto any bill that does not appear to follow the Iranian Constitution. In the 2005 presidential elections, the council banned all but six of more than one thousand possible candidates. All female candidates were banned, even

Tehran: Iran's Capital City

Tehran, the capital of Iran, sits in the shadow of the Alborz Mountains. It is a busy, bustling city, home to about 8.5 million people. Cars and motorcycles clog the streets, spewing pollution into the air. The mountains trap the dirty air over the city, so that Tehran is often covered in a thick smog.

People have been living in what is now Tehran for eight thousand years. In early times, the city on this site was known as Ray. Tehran was first mentioned in the eleventh century. The city grew into an important trade center, and in the late 1700s, its population began to explode. Tehran became the capital of Iran in 1795.

Today, Tehran is the economic and educational center of Iran. The city is a mix of modern buildings and lovely gardens. Its most famous landmark is the Azadi Tower, a white marble monument built in 1971 that echoes traditional Iranian architecture. Other sites include the Golestan Palace, once the home of the leaders of the Qajar dynasty, and the National Museum of Iran, which features displays ranging from ancient artifacts to modern pottery. Tehran is also home to the National Jewels Museum, which houses the crown jewels of Iran. The largest jewelry collection in the world, it includes emeralds, rubies, diamonds, and sapphires, and decorated swords, tiaras, and thrones.

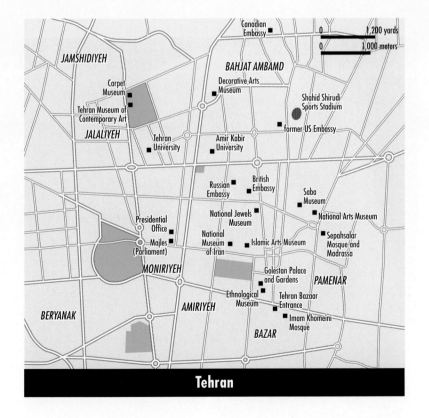

though Iran's constitution does not bar women from holding political office.

The Supreme Defense Council (SDC) is a military group charged with planning the military and defense policies of Iran. The supreme leader has the power to appoint or remove military leaders who serve on the council. The SDC may recommend military action, but it is the supreme leader who can declare war.

The Supreme Leader

The supreme leader is the most powerful person in Iran. He is both head of the government and Iran's most powerful Islamic

Saeed Jalili became secretary of the Supreme Defense Council in 2007.

authority. The supreme leader must be one of the nation's highest-ranking clerics, who have the title of grand ayatollah.

The supreme leader's primary job is to make sure that all branches of the government function in accordance with the

The supreme leader (in brown robe) works closely with other government officials.

Sayyed Ali Khamenei

Ayatollah Sayyed Ali Khamenei (1939–) has been Iran's supreme leader since 1989. Among Khamenei's main policies are promoting his vision of the revolutionary ideals of the first supreme leader, Khomeini. These include social conservatism and a strong authoritarian government. The revolutionary ideals strive to reduce westernization in Iranian society, but this has proven difficult. For example, the rise of the Internet and satellite radio and television is a major obstacle to reducing Western cultural influence on Iranians.

Ahmad Jannati (in blue robe) has been the leader of the Guardian Council since 1988.

basic beliefs of Islam. The supreme leader can declare war or peace. He appoints the head of Iran's Supreme Court, six members of the Guardian Council, and all commanders of the

Mahmoud Ahmadinejad

Iran's president, Mahmoud Ahmadinejad (1956–), is a conservative former mayor of Tehran. He was elected first in 2005 and again in 2009. Ahmadinejad has been praised for improving the economy and reducing unemployment, but he also has controversial ideas. He claims that the Holocaust—the systematic murder of millions of Jews, Roma (Gypsies), disabled people, and others during World War II—did not happen. He also refuses to acknowledge the legitimacy of the state of Israel.

armed forces. He also determines leaders of Friday prayer and the heads of Iran's state-run media.

The Executive

The second-highest-ranking official in Iran is the president. Elected for four-year terms, presidents can only serve two consecutive terms. The president's main responsibility is to make sure that Iran's constitution is upheld and its laws followed. The

Mohammad Khatami served as president from 1997 until 2005.

Iran's National Government

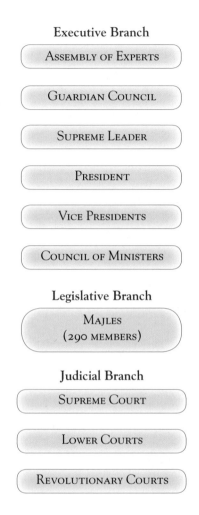

Executive Branch

- ASSEMBLY OF EXPERTS
- GUARDIAN COUNCIL
- SUPREME LEADER
- PRESIDENT
- VICE PRESIDENTS
- COUNCIL OF MINISTERS

Legislative Branch

- MAJLES (290 MEMBERS)

Judicial Branch

- SUPREME COURT
- LOWER COURTS
- REVOLUTIONARY COURTS

president answers to the supreme leader. People who wish to run for president must be approved by the Guardian Council.

The president also has a cabinet called the Council of Ministers. Each minister is chosen by the president and approved by the legislature. There are only two clerics and no women among the current ministers, who supervise such areas as housing, defense, roads and transportation, health, and education.

Iran has five vice presidents, each with different responsibilities. The first vice president is responsible for the activities of the Council of Ministers. The other vice presidents are in charge of specific departments, such as atomic energy or environmental planning.

President Mahmoud Ahmadinejad walks with his vice presidents.

Iran's Flag

Iran's flag has three horizontal bands: green on the top, white in the middle, and red on the bottom. In the center is a red version of a tulip, a symbol of martyrdom, or giving one's life for a cause. The tulip is also a representation of the word *Allah*, which means "God" in Arabic. In white Arabic script on the central border, the phrase *Allah akbar* (God is great) is repeated. The green on the flag represents growth and the connection to Islam. White represents honesty and peace. Red stands for bravery. The flag was adopted after the Islamic Revolution in 1979 and is a slight variation of the flag used under the ousted shah.

The Majles

The Majles is Iran's legislature, or parliament. Its 290 members are elected every four years. The Majles writes and passes laws, approves appointed ministers, and can remove the president or ministers if those officials do anything against Iran's constitution.

Lawmakers in Iran are conservative, reformist, or radical. Conservatives often come from the Muslim clergy or from the bazaar merchants. They support ideas such as strict dress codes and controlling what can be broadcast on radio or television. The reformists are mostly middle-class professionals and wealthy business owners. They want to change the government from within. They are open to foreign ideas and have a more relaxed attitude toward social and cultural issues, like the role of women in society and Iran's relationships with other nations. The radicals or revolutionaries support government control of industry, social programs to help all citizens, and fair methods of distributing the nation's wealth. Both the radicals and conservatives oppose close contact with Western cultures.

The Courts

Iran's judiciary includes a supreme court, lower courts, and revolutionary courts. The head justice and the chief prosecutor are required to be specialists in shari'a, the basic legal ideas of Islamic law. The supreme court deals with major crimes or questions involving Iran's constitution. Lower courts deal with lesser or local crimes, such as car theft or burglary. Revolutionary courts try people accused of smuggling, violations of religious norms, treason against the Iranian government, or stirring up violence. Such crimes include speaking out against the government or against Islam.

Iran's National Anthem

In 1989, Iran held a contest for a new national anthem. The music for the anthem that won was written by Hassan Riyahi. The new anthem was adopted in 1990.

Upwards on the horizon rises the Eastern Sun,
The sight of the true Religion.
Bahman—the brilliance of our Faith,
Your message, O Imam, of independence and freedom
Is imprinted on our souls.
O Martyrs! The time of your cries of pain rings in our ears,
Enduring, continuing, eternal,
The Islamic Republic of Iran.

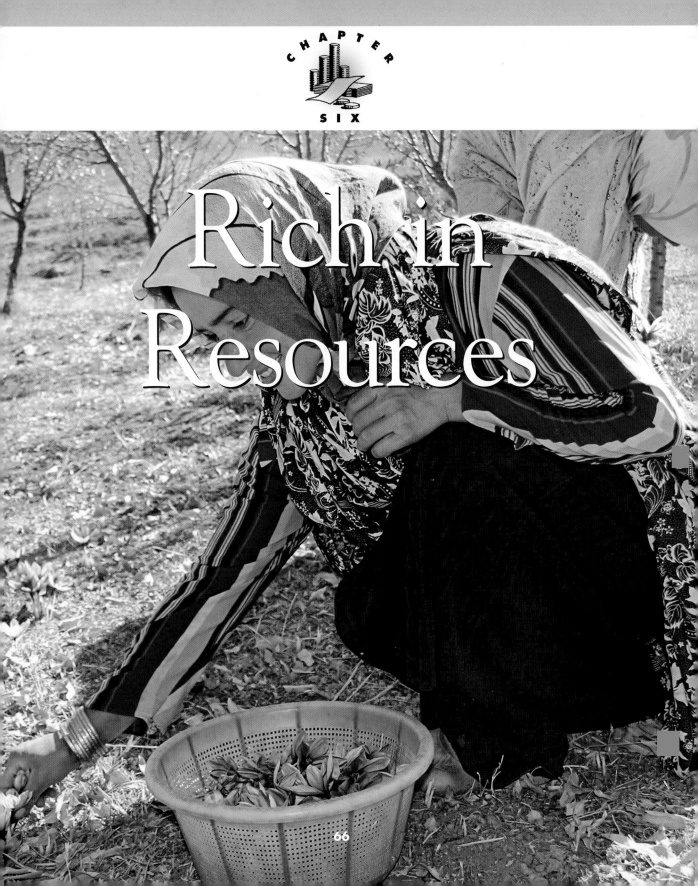

CHAPTER

SIX

Rich in Resources

BAHAR'S FAMILY WORKS IN THE SAFFRON TRADE IN the northeastern town of Ghaen. Saffron is a spice that comes from parts of the saffron crocus flower, and collecting it is hard work. Iran produces 94 percent of the world's saffron, which is used in rice dishes and as a yellow dye. Although she is just thirteen, Bahar has been picking and processing crocus flowers for this vivid yellow spice for five years. Her family needs her to work to help with the family's expenses.

Ten-year-old Raheem is an apprentice rug maker in the ancient city of Tabriz. He began learning the art of hand-knotting Persian carpets when he was seven. It will be many years before he becomes a master and makes carpets on his own. Until then, he will learn how to dye yarn, form knots, and follow the patterns that make Iran famous for its hand-woven carpets.

Bahar and Raheem are among the thousands of Iranian children who work to help out their families. They work because many Iranian families struggle to make ends meet. The minimum age for working in Iran is fifteen, but that is

Opposite: **Harvesting saffron requires picking crocus flowers by hand.**

Making carpets is difficult and time-consuming.

often ignored. Small businesses, family-owned retail shops, bazaar stalls, and farms put children to work at an early age. About 62 percent of child workers are girls. Most child labor is in the carpet industry and farming.

Iran's Economy

Politics, technology, unemployment, and inflation affect Iran's growing economy. The politics of the country's leaders affects international trade. Iran's government leaders do not want their citizens to have much contact with Western culture. This, along with economic sanctions that the United States and other nations placed on Iran, means that Iran is isolated from the places where it could sell its products.

Farming has traditionally been a major part of the economy. But the country has limited access to advanced agricultural technology. Much of the equipment used in farming, mining, and manufacturing is old.

Agriculture employs one-fourth of all Iranian workers and accounts for 11 percent of the economy. Manufacturing and mining make up one-third of the economy, and the rest of the labor force works in services. This includes fields such as health care, education, and restaurants.

Another factor affecting Iran's economy is the high unemployment rate. In 2010, nearly 15 percent of Iranians of working age did not have jobs. Most unemployed Iranians are unskilled workers. Iran has a serious shortage of skilled workers and workers with experience in modern technology. There are too few people with the necessary knowledge and experience for high-tech, health care, and industrial work.

Most Iranians work six days a week and eight hours a day. The average workweek is forty-eight hours. The traditional day off is Friday, the day when Muslims attend prayer services in their local mosques. All workers are given time during the day to answer the call to prayer.

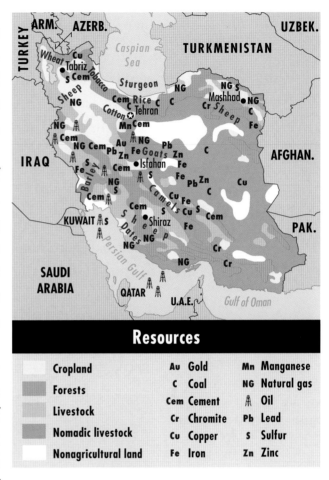

Resources

Cropland	Au	Gold	Mn	Manganese
Forests	C	Coal	NG	Natural gas
Livestock	Cem	Cement	Oil	Oil
Nomadic livestock	Cr	Chromite	Pb	Lead
Nonagricultural land	Cu	Copper	S	Sulfur
	Fe	Iron	Zn	Zinc

Farming, Forestry, and Fishing

One-fourth of Iran's land is suitable for farming, but not all of this land is actually farmed. The problem is water. Iran's relative lack of freshwater means that only some farmland can be irrigated, or watered, regularly. Irrigation dramatically increases crop yields, such as Iran's wheat crop, for example. Two-fifths of the land dedicated to growing wheat is irrigated, while the rest is watered only by rain. The irrigated region produces more than twice as much wheat as the larger, rain-fed area. There simply isn't enough freshwater for Iranians to irrigate all of their farmland.

Because Iran's climate varies greatly, the nation can produce a wide range of agricultural products. Grains, including wheat, barley, rice, and corn, are raised in all regions except the deserts. Fruits produced in Iran range from dates, which

Harvest season is one of the busiest times of the year for farmworkers.

In 2010, Iran produced half of the world's pistachios.

grow in desert oases, to melons, which grow in the sandy southern soil. Orchards produce peaches and apricots, while vineyards produce table grapes and several types of raisins. Pistachios, almonds, and walnuts grow in the wild in Iran, and are also raised in well-tended orchards. Iran produces more

What Does It Cost?

Here are some prices for common items in Iran:

Item	Iran Price	U.S. Equivalent
Three-course dinner	70,000 to 90,000 rials + tip	$6.61 to $8.50
(soup, meat and salad, fruit)		
Double hamburger	10,000 rials	$0.95
Iranian pizza	20,000 rials	$1.89
Local bus ticket	200 rials	$0.02
Movie ticket	5,000 to 10,000 rials	$0.47 to $0.94
Breakfast in a four-star restaurant	44,000 to 66,000 rials	$4.16 to $6.24

Sheep produce wool that can be used to make clothing, blankets, and other goods.

pistachios than any other nation in the world and comes in second in the production of apricots and dates.

Many farmers raise livestock. Sheep and goats are most common, followed by cattle, donkeys, horses, water buffalo, and mules. Lack of water and limited grain to feed livestock limits the types of animals raised. Sheep and goats can graze on wild grasses and shrubs, while beef cattle need more food and water to survive. Iranian farmers also produce chickens, eggs, milk, cheese, and butter.

About 11 percent of Iran is forested. Oak, elm, poplar, maple, and walnut are woods used for furniture. Pines and cedars are used in construction and some furniture making, as well as in the production of fiberboard and plywood. Drought and forest fires have destroyed large areas of forested land, reducing timber resources. Between 1954 and 2004, Iran lost

What Iran Grows, Makes, and Mines

Agriculture (2010)

Wheat	15 million metric tons
Rice	2.8 million metric tons
Pistachio nuts	230,000 metric tons

Manufacturing (2010)

Cars and trucks	1.6 million vehicles produced
Motorcycles	1 million units produced
Handmade rugs	US$420 million in exports

Mining (2006)

Petroleum	4.17 million barrels/day
Natural gas	200 billion cubic meters
Iron ore	33 million metric tons

two-fifths of its forests to drought and fire. Today, the office of the Environmental Protection Organization (EPO) controls cutting trees and replanting forests.

The EPO also manages Iran's commercial fishing industry. Most of the commercial fishing takes place in the Caspian Sea and the Persian Gulf. Iranian fishers take bream, whitefish, salmon, mullet, carp, perch, and loach from the Caspian Sea. Iran has a reputation for selling fine caviar, the fish eggs of sturgeon. Fishers also target the 150 edible species that live in the Persian Gulf. Fifty-two percent of the fish caught in Iran come from the Persian Gulf. Shrimp and prawns are popular, along with oysters, needlefish, catfish, flathead, and grouper. Iran processes fish by canning, smoking, and salting. Processed fish is sold in Iran and exported to other countries.

Mining

Iran's greatest wealth lies in its petroleum and natural gas reserves. The National Iranian Oil Company (NIOC), which is run by the government, produces all petroleum products in Iran. The NIOC is the world's second-largest oil company, producing more than four million barrels of petroleum per day. Natural gas production stands at 200 billion cubic meters a day. About one-fourth of mining workers are in the petroleum industry.

Some oil rigs are located in the Persian Gulf off the Iranian coast.

Iran is currently the eighth-largest producer of iron worldwide. Much of the iron is exported to China. Other important metals mined in Iran include copper, lead, zinc, barite, and bauxite. Iran also produces some silver and gold.

Industrial materials make up a large part of the mining industry. Iran produces 50 million tons (45 million metric tons) of cement yearly for the construction industry. Iranian gypsum is used in plaster and fertilizer. Soda ash and silica are essential ingredients in making glass, while Iran's kaolin is used to make fine china.

Mining is difficult and dangerous work.

The Rial vs. the Toman

In a Tehran street, cab fare is listed as 5,000 rials, but the cab driver might say, "That costs 500 tomans." A toman is worth 10 rials. With inflation so high, using tomans is easier for both buyers and sellers. One hundred dinars make one rial, but people rarely deal in dinars.

Rials come in both coins and banknotes. Coins worth 250, 500, and 1,000 rials are common. Less common are those worth 50, 100, 2,000, and 5,000 rials. Banknotes are available in values of 100, 200, 500, 1,000, 2,000, 5,000, 10,000, 20,000, 50,000, and 100,000 rials. The current 100,000 rial note has a picture of the Ayatollah Khomeini on the front and the tomb of the poet Sa'di on the back. In 2011, 100,000 rials was worth US$9.45. The Iranian government plans to remove three zeros from the currency, which means 100,000 rials would instead be 100 rials.

Precious and semiprecious gemstones are found in Iran. Iranians mine emeralds, sapphires, and rubies. Natural pearls are taken from oysters in the Persian Gulf. Semiprecious gems found in Iran include amber, turquoise, and opals. Jewelers consider turquoise from Iran to be the finest in the world.

Turquoise and other valuable stones are often used to decorate mosques.

Manufacturing

Iran manufactures petroleum products, automobiles, trucks, textiles, processed food, and electronic appliances. The petroleum industry is the nation's largest and most profitable industry. It employs people in many different jobs. People in the petroleum industry work at oil and natural gas wells, and they work at refineries. They drive tanker trucks and sell oil.

The automotive industry is the nation's second-largest industry. Iran makes cars, trucks, motorcycles, minibuses, tractors, and road construction equipment. Iran made 1.6 million cars and 1 million motorcycles in 2010. The most popular car model in the country, the Pride, costs about 7,150,000 tomans (US$6,757). While this may seem inexpensive, the average

Iran Khodro is the largest Iranian automobile manufacturer.

Magic Carpets

Carpets are among the most beautiful crafts of Iran. There are more than one million weavers in Iran, each producing unique handwoven carpets. Iran exports $420 million worth of carpets, or about three-fourths of the world's market. The yarns are hand dyed, and rugs are woven from wool, silk, or cotton. Specific carpet centers have developed patterns that are named for the cities from which they come. Popular patterns include Bakhtiari, Isfahan, Qum, Tabriz, Heriz, and Shiraz.

Iranian's monthly income is only about US$500. With the costs of food, fuel, and housing increasing rapidly, few Iranians can afford a new car.

The textile industry covers a wide range of jobs and products. Workers process raw cotton, wool, or silk into yarn. Some weave fabric on machines, though Iran prides itself on its handmade carpets. Iranians collect and process the raw materials needed for textiles, as well as manufacture the goods. Clothing, upholstery fabrics, draperies, bedding, and bath linens are produced and sold in Iran, while rugs are sold worldwide.

Food processing converts raw, fresh foods into foods that last on the shelf. Iranians can, salt, or smoke sardines, herring, and tuna. They process sugar beets into granulated sugar and produce millions of gallons of fruit juice and sodas. Millions of tons of vegetable oil is processed each year.

Tehran is the industrial center of Iran. Nearly half of all industrial workers and nearly all major corporations have factories and offices in Tehran. Since Iran's government owns many major corporations, nearly half of all Iranians work for the government.

Transportation

Iran maintains a large network of roads and transportation hubs. Although bus or train fare is cheap, most Iranians travel by car. This has led to serious smog problems in Iran's major cities. The government encourages people to take public transportation, but many Iranians like the independence of traveling in their own vehicles.

Railways are owned and operated by the government. The main railway line connects the Caspian Sea to the Persian Gulf. There are small branch lines between the main line and provincial capitals. Trains are used for personal transportation, but the majority of train traffic is from carrying products from one city to another.

Driving in Tehran

Visitors to Tehran who plan to drive in the city need to know the laws—or the lack of them. Red lights in Iran are considered more of a suggestion than a command to stop. Traffic signs are followed when it is convenient. Drivers are supposed to stay to the right and pass only if there is room. In the cities, drivers are more likely to just keep going rather than yield the right-of-way. People unfamiliar with Iran's driving habits are usually advised to take a taxi. It is much safer.

Rich in Resources **79**

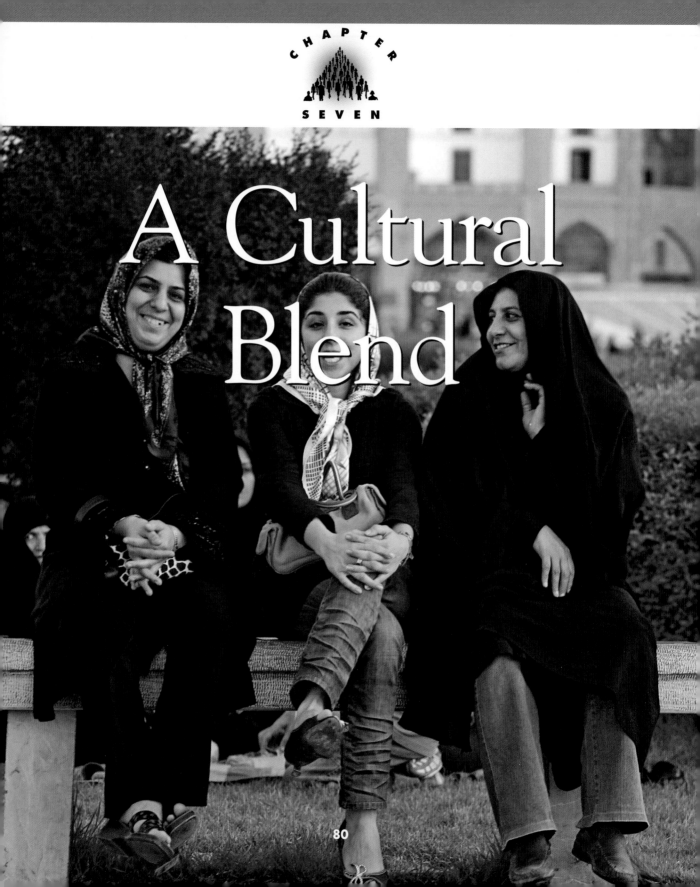

A Cultural Blend

REZIN, JAFAR, AND MAHMOUD ARE IRANIAN TEENS. They are all thirteen, but their backgrounds and lives are very different. Rezin lives in the northwestern mountains. The daughter of a Kurdish shepherd, Rezin does not go to school. She helps her mother care for her four younger brothers and works with the family's herd. Rezin helps deliver lambs, shear sheep, clean wool, and deliver wool to the local market. In Tabriz, Jafar, the son of an Azeri merchant, attends a *rahnamayi*, a middle school. He is a technology whiz and hopes to study computer science in technical school. Mahmoud's father is a petroleum engineer in Tehran. Mahmoud attends a private school where he learns French, German, and computer technology.

Opposite: **Young people relaxing in Isfahan's Meidan-e Imam Square**

Young and Urban

Iran's population is growing and changing more rapidly than most other nations. The population is estimated at 76,923,300 as of 2010, but nearly 70 percent of those people are less than thirty years old. One-fourth of Iran's population is fifteen years old or younger.

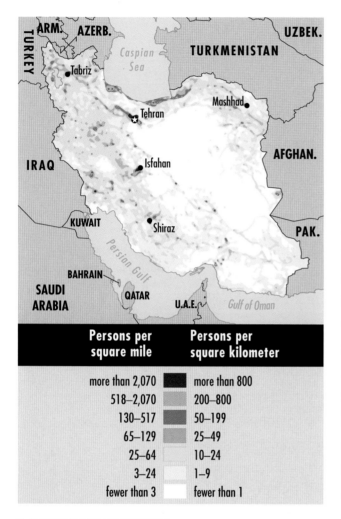

Persons per square mile		Persons per square kilometer
more than 2,070		more than 800
518–2,070		200–800
130–517		50–199
65–129		25–49
25–64		10–24
3–24		1–9
fewer than 3		fewer than 1

Population in major cities (2010 est.)

Tehran	8,429,807
Mashhad	2,965,000
Shiraz	1,750,000
Tabriz	1,698,000
Isfahan	1,630,000

In 1950, most Iranians lived in rural areas, mainly on farms and in small villages. In the 1960s, people began moving into the cities and leaving farm life behind. Today, 60 percent of Iranians live in cities.

The Islamic Revolution brought a major change to Iran's population. Immediately after the revolution, many educated professionals—such as doctors, lawyers, writers, and engineers—left Iran because they did not want to live under Islamic rule. They moved to the United States, Canada, Australia, and various European countries. At present, five million Iranians live in foreign countries. Many Jews and followers of the Baha'i faith were among those who left. They were concerned that they would suffer persecution under Iran's new Islamic government. At the same time, Iran has become home to many refugees. Large numbers of Arabs and Kurds have moved into Iran from Iraq and Afghanistan.

Cities and Towns

Iranian cities are laid out in quarters. The business quarter is where the bazaar is located, although modern business centers have sprung up next to the traditional bazaar alleyways. A central plaza, a mosque, and perhaps a public garden are found near the maze of corridors that make up the bazaar. Government offices and residential neighborhoods are in other sections of the city.

In most small cities, people live in traditional mud-brick or stone homes with central courtyards and gardens. In Tehran, Tabriz, and Mashhad, modern apartment buildings provide

Mud-brick buildings stay cool in the heat.

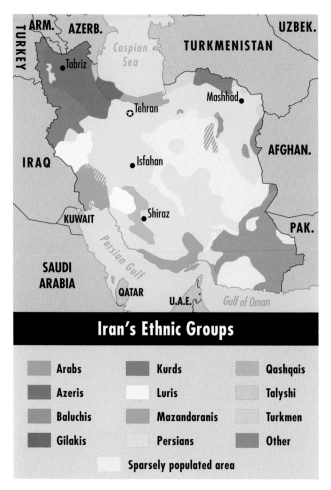

Iran's Ethnic Groups

Arabs	Kurds	Qashqais
Azeris	Luris	Talyshi
Baluchis	Mazandaranis	Turkmen
Gilakis	Persians	Other

Sparsely populated area

Ethnic Representation

Persian	51%
Azeri	24%
Gilaki and Mazandarani	8%
Kurd	7%
Arab	3%
Lurs	2%
Baloch	2%
Turkmen	2%
Other	1%

most housing for families. Few young adults live in their own apartments. Instead, they usually remain in the family home until they marry. Only the wealthy can afford a house in Tehran.

Most rural towns are near water sources. Mountain towns are carved into the rocky slopes, and most houses are made of mud-brick, with few windows and a ventilation hole in the roof. Communities that have sprung up beside oases have a different style of housing. Many of these people's ancestors once lived as nomads. They live in round or cone-shaped huts or heavy-duty tents.

Ethnic Mix

Slightly more than half of Iranians speak Persian as their primary language and are considered ethnic Persians. The rest of Iran's population is made up of large and diverse populations, including Azeris, Armenians, Kurds, and Arabs. The Azeris represent nearly one-fourth of Iran's population. Many Azeris work on farms or raise sheep or goats, and live in the northwestern region of Iran, near Azerbaijan. Gilakis and Mazandaranis live in the coastal region of the Caspian Sea, where most earn their livings as farmers or fishermen. About eight million Kurds live in the mountains along the Iran-Iraq border. In ancient times, the word *Kurd* referred to nomadic herders. Arabs constitute 3 percent of Iran's population and are concentrated in southwestern Iran, in Khuzistan Province, which is located on the border with Iraq and Kuwait.

Iranian Languages

Iran's official language is Persian, which is called Farsi in the Persian language. There are many dialects, or regional varieties, of Persian. It is written using an Arabic-style alphabet. More than half of Iranians speak Persian. All schoolchildren learn Persian, so even those who speak a different primary language can speak and read the language. Persian is the language used by the government, on television and radio, in newspapers and movies, and on the Internet.

Many Iranians buy daily newspapers from newsstands in bazaars.

How do you say . . .

Pronouncing Persian is fairly easy. *A* and *e* are short vowel sounds, as in *pat* and *pet*. *I* sounds like a long *e*, as in *see*. *O* is a long *o*, as in *oak*, and *u* is a long *u*, as in *duke*. The combination *kh* is a guttural *ch*, as in *loch*, and *aa* is pronounced as a short *o*, as in *pot*.

salaam	hello
khodaa-haafez	good-bye
khaahesh meekenam	please
mersee	thank you
baleh	yes
nakheyr	no
ma'zerat meekhaaham	excuse me
sobh-bekheyr	good morning
Hal-e shoman chetoreh?	How are you?
khoobam, mersee	fine, thank you

Iranians speak dozens of different languages. Persian is the most common.

Other languages spoken in Iran include Kurdish, Arabic, and Azeri Turkish. Kurdish is spoken along the western Zagros Mountains. Arabic is an important language in Iran because Arabic is the language of the Qur'an.

About 7 percent of the Iranian population is Kurdish.

Common Languages in Iran

Persian and Persian dialects	58%
Turkic and Turkic dialects	26%
Kurdish	9%
Luri	2%
Balochi	1%
Arabic	1%
Turkish	1%
Other	2%

A Cultural Blend **87**

Children in Iran are required to attend school from ages six to fourteen.

Literacy

The literacy rate is the percentage of people over fifteen years old who can read and write. In Iran, 83.5 percent of men and 70.4 percent of women are literate.

School Days

Iranian children begin school at age four, with a year of preschool, which is much like kindergarten. Primary school covers grades one through five, ages five through eleven. Students then move into middle school for three years. The future direction of a student's education is determined during the first year of upper secondary school, which is like high school. There are three levels of upper secondary school, including academic, technical/vocational, and *Kar-danesh*. Academic high school leads to college. Four-year technical or vocational schools train students in services, agriculture, and industry. Kar-danesh is a two-year vocational program, ending in a license to pursue work in farming, industry, or services.

Boys and girls attend separate schools, and all children wear uniforms. School is Saturday through Thursday, and students attend two hundred days per year. School is not held on Fridays or on national and religious holidays. In school, children study reading, writing, math, sciences, history, geography, English, and Arabic.

Getting into college depends on scoring well on the Konkur, the Iranian college entrance exam. The exam is hard, and only 10 percent of those who take it enter college. A college degree is no guarantee of a job. One in ten young people who are unemployed have college degrees. Because unemployment is so high, more than 150,000 educated Iranians move to other countries for jobs. They see no future for themselves in Iran.

Students must do well on the Konkur to be admitted to a college.

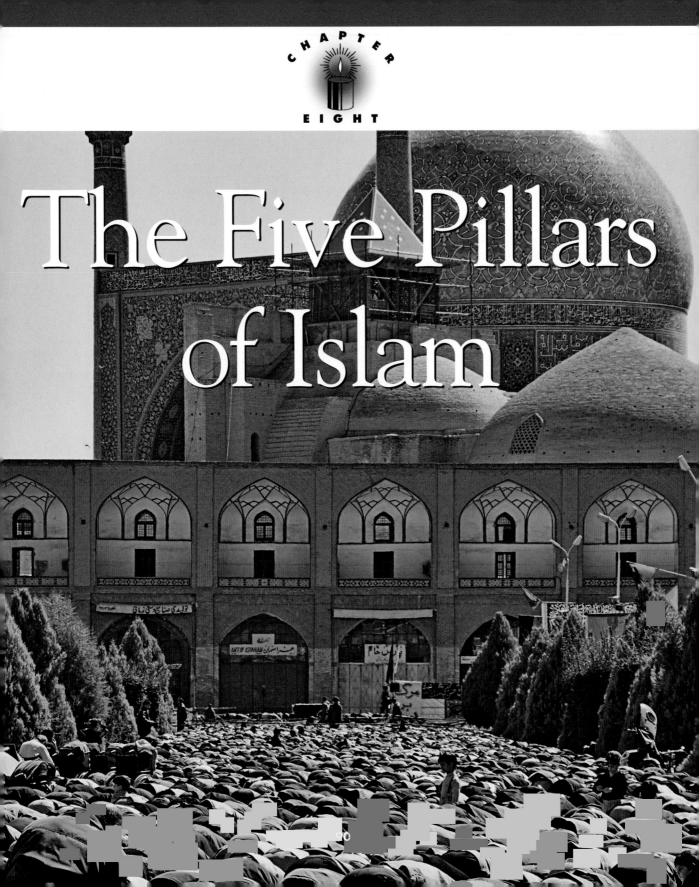

The Five Pillars of Islam

A<small>T DAWN, A MUEZZIN'S VOICE REACHES OUT FROM</small> the minaret, or tower, of a mosque across the city of Shiraz. The muezzin is calling faithful Muslims to prayer. Hashem rises and washes. He kneels down on his prayer rugs facing in the direction of the holy city of Mecca. Lowering his forehead to the ground, he begins to pray. This is the first of three times Hashem will pray throughout the day. Prayer is an important part of the lives of all Muslims.

The official religion of Iran is Shi'i Islam, one of the two major sects of Islam. The other is Sunni Islam. Ninety-eight percent of Iran's population follow Islam. Of that number, 95 percent are Shi'i. The remaining 2 percent of the population are Christian, Jewish, Zoroastrian, Mandaean, Yarsani, and Baha'i. According to Iran's constitution, Christianity, Judaism, and Zoroastrianism are officially recognized religions, and their followers are allowed to pursue their own beliefs.

Opposite: **Muslims gather together every Friday at midday for a special prayer.**

Shi'i and Sunni

The division between Shi'is and Sunnis can be traced to the death of the Prophet Muhammad in 632 CE. When

Imams lead religious services and answer questions about Islam.

Religions in Iran

Shi'i Muslim	89%
Sunni Muslim	9%
Christian	0.3%
Jewish	0.05%
Zoroastrian	0.03%

Less than 1 percent of Iranians follow the Baha'i faith, a faith not recognized as a religion by the Iranian government.

Muhammad died, Islam needed a new leader. Those who followed the Prophet Muhammad's son-in-law Ali and daughter Fatimah were called Sh'i-t Ali, or "the partisans of Ali." Today, they are known as Shi'i Muslims. They call Ali and his successors imams.

Those who chose to accept Muhammad's close ally, Abu Bakr, and the others who later succeeded him as leader eventually came to be called the people of the Sunnah and Jama'ah—which means "people of the Tradition and Consensus," or Sunni for short. Shi'is believe that imams are chosen by Allah and are sinless. Sunnis believe that any member of the Arab Quraysh tribe could become the religious leader, called a caliph.

Sunni Muslims demonstrating against Shi'i Muslims

Thousands of people travel to Mecca each year.

The Five Pillars

All Muslims must fulfill five duties, called the Five Pillars of Islam, to live good lives.

- *Shahadah:* A Muslim must make a declaration of faith by saying, "There is no god but God, and Muhammad is the messenger of God."
- *Salah:* Muslims pray five times a day—at dawn, midday, late afternoon, at sunset, and before going to bed. Some Muslims perform these prayers only three times: at sunrise,

Ramadan

The month of Ramadan is a thirty-day period of fasting. Adult Muslims do not eat or drink anything during the daylight hours. This is a period of sacrifice in an attempt to become closer to God. Ramadan is a time for doing good deeds, being generous to the poor, and reading the Qur'an. People who are sick or traveling and women who are pregnant or nursing are not expected to fast. Because the Islamic calendar is based on a lunar year rather than a solar year, the date of Ramadan shifts by about ten days each year. At the end of Ramadan, fasters enjoy 'Id al-Fitr, a celebration of the end of the fast.

noon, and sundown. Shi'is in particular combine prayers into three sessions. Prayers are said in three positions: standing, bowing down, and prostrating (touching the forehead to the ground). Muslims wash before prayer.

- *Zakat:* Muslims are required to donate to charity. Every Muslim gives money or food to the poor and needy, or for religious purposes, as part of zakat, the act of purifying or cleansing the soul. Zakat allows a Muslim to do away with selfishness or greed.

- *Sawm:* During the holy month of Ramadan, the ninth month of the Islamic calendar, Muslims fast from sunrise to sunset.

- *Hajj:* Muslims must make a pilgrimage to Mecca at least once during their lives, if they are physically and financially able to do so.

Muslims follow the teachings set down in the Qur'an, the holy book of Islam. According to tradition, Allah had the angel Gabriel teach the Prophet Muhammad the text of the Qur'an in the years 610 to 632 CE. Muhammad's closest followers memorized, recited, and recorded the contents of each chapter.

After the Prophet Muhammad died in 632, the new Muslim leaders collected the chapters into a single book.

Religious Holidays in Iran

Iran's religious holidays follow the Islamic lunar calendar, which has 354 or 355 days in a year. On a Western calendar, Islamic holidays move forward 10 to 11 days each year.

Holiday

Tasu'a
Ashura (right)
Death of the Prophet Muhammad
Death of the Imam Reza
Birthday of the Prophet Muhammad
Anniversary of the death of Fatimah
Birthday of Imam Ali
Mission of Muhammad
Birthday of Imam Mahdi
Death of Imam Ali
'Id al-Fitr
Death of Imam Jafar Sadegh
'Id al-Adha
Qadir-e Khom

Iran's mosques are beautiful works of art and architecture. When visiting a mosque, people should follow some basic rules. All people must remove their shoes as they enter the mosque. There is an area for storing shoes, and it is important to never walk on a prayer carpet in shoes. Women must be covered from ankle to neck and wear scarves on their heads. Men should wear long pants and a buttoned shirt. Jeans and T-shirts are not appropriate.

Non-Muslims should plan to visit a mosque when it is not a time of prayer. Mosques usually have programs to welcome visiting non-Muslims. Do not talk loudly or take photos of people without their permission.

The Qur'an contains 114 chapters that are further divided into verses.

Other Religions

Zoroastrians are the followers of Zarathustra. They believe in one god and follow the teachings written in the Avesta. There are ten thousand Mandaeans in Iran. They believe in Old Testament leaders, including Adam, Moses, and Noah. Yarsani believe in the rebirth of great religious leaders. The angel Gabriel, for example, is believed to have been reborn as the prophet Benjamin of the Old Testament.

While Christianity, Judaism, and Zoroastrianism are tolerated by the Iranian government, this does not mean that

An estimated three hundred thousand Christians live in Iran.

members of these religions do not experience discrimination. For example, they do not have equal access to positions of power in the political, military, or security branches of government. Discrimination against them is often not explicitly outlawed. More importantly, the government does not usually enforce the laws that do protect them from discrimination.

Jews and Baha'is face the greatest difficulty. Iran is home to the largest Middle Eastern Jewish community outside of Israel and the West Bank. The constant political tensions between Iran and Israel periodically cause crises in which Jewish Iranians are accused of spying. The Baha'i faith emerged among Shi'is in Iran in the nineteenth century, so the Shi'i religious establishment simply considers it to be an incorrect version of Shi'i Islam. Therefore, they allow and endorse systematic discrimination and persecution of Baha'is.

About twenty-five thousand Jewish people live in Iran.

CHAPTER NINE

The Arts and More

N AVEED AND HIS FRIENDS ARE HEADED TO VAN IN
western Turkey. They are going to a concert by Iranian rock artists
who now live in the United States. The star is Andy Madadian,
better known to Iranian teens as just Andy. Every year, Andy and
other Iranian singers and musicians head to cities along Iran's
border in Turkey, Dubai, and Armenia. They play music that is
illegal in Iran, but listened to over the Internet by Iranian teens.

Iran has a rich cultural heritage dating back more than two
thousand years. The stunning architecture of mosques, palaces,
and museums is evident throughout the country. However, music,
theater, television, art, and literature are controlled under Iran's
national laws, which are influenced by Islamic rules of behavior.
Art that clerics do not approve of is not allowed. Even in sports,
Islamic norms are sometimes enforced by the state. Women and
girls who participate in sports must do so with their heads and
bodies fully covered.

Opposite: **Iranian rock and pop groups, such as Arian, perform shows around the world.**

Architecture

Iran's most ancient buildings are a testament to their architectural skills. The remains of Persepolis—the ancient capital of

Artifacts from Persepolis are now in museums around the world.

the Achaemenian Empire built by Darius I in 518 BCE—feature huge wall carvings, slender columns, and a sculpture of Darius. At one time, the sculptures at Persepolis were covered with gold, silver, and bright blue lapis lazuli stone.

Another impressive site is Chogha Zanbil, the holy city of the Elamite kingdom, which was built around 1250 BCE. The city featured three concentric walls. The ziggurat, a temple in the shape of a pyramid, was the largest in the region.

After the arrival of the Arabs and Islam, the architectural skills of Iranians were also used to build mosques, tombs, and shrines for imams. Islamic monuments feature intricate tile work, gold, and decorative calligraphy. Many mosques have stylish domes and minarets, open courtyards, and beautifully designed gardens. Among the most stunning mosques are the Jameh Mosque in Hamadan, the Sheikh Lotf Allah Mosque in Isfahan, and the Goharshad Mosque in Mashhad.

Visual Arts

Iran's traditional arts are best represented by the country's handcrafts. Handmade rugs are works of art. They feature repeating patterns of flowers, medallions, and geometric figures. Mosaics, made from handmade tiles, add color and pattern to buildings and fountains. The most popular color has traditionally been blue, duplicating the semiprecious stones of turquoise and lapis lazuli. Calligraphy, the art of handwriting, has been a traditional art since Zoroastrian times. Calligraphy was used to decorate books, mosques, and shrines. Modern

The Blue Mosque

Construction of the Blue Mosque in Tabriz began in 1465 CE, but it took another twenty-five years to decorate. It was destroyed in an earthquake in 1773 but was later reconstructed. The surface of the mosque is mostly covered with tiles in a range of blues, from palest turquoise to a rich royal blue. Other surfaces feature beautiful calligraphy. The main entryway is typical of the intricate tile work found on many mosques and palaces throughout Iran.

Khatam-kari

Khatam-kari is the complex art of encrusting artworks with intricate patterns. Jewelry boxes, chessboards, tables, desks, frames, clocks, and musical instruments may feature khatam-kari decorations. More than 250 pieces of metal, bone, ivory, and wood produce 0.15 square inch (1 sq cm) of khatam-kari decoration. The art of khatam-kari was popular during the Safavid era (the 1500s) in southern Iran.

calligraphy by artists such as Charles Hossein Zenderoudi and Parviz Tanavoli appear in contemporary artwork seen in today's Iranian art galleries.

Modern art became popular in Iran in the late 1940s and early 1950s. Artists such as Marcos Grigorian and Abbas Attar made an international impact on Iran's artistic reputation. Grigorian led a group of painters and sculptors in Tehran in the 1970s. He created artworks made of clay and straw, many of which are on display in the Tehran Museum of Contemporary Art. Abbas, a photographer, is known for photojournalism. His book *Iran Diary* is a photo essay on life in Iran from 1971 to 2002.

Theater

Iran has several types of traditional theater, from classical drama to operas to comedies. Depicting heroic events from history has been common in Iranian theater for centuries. In the *ruhozi* performance tradition, the actors set up a stage in the yard of a house and perform for the guests. When the Islamic republic was established, most Iranian theater groups closed down. Two theater forms that survived are *ta'zieh* and puppet theater.

Ta'zieh is Iran's religious and dramatic musical theater. Presentations include singing and playing instruments, reciting poetry and other works, and performing dramas. In Arabic, *ta'zieh* means "mourning rituals." It commemorates Shi'i imams and martyrs. Ta'ziehs became popular in the nineteenth century. Typical topics for ta'zieh plays are the struggles or deaths of imams or other holy figures who fought against evil.

Ta'ziehs are often performed on the holy day of Ashura.

Saman Salour has won several awards for his films.

Iranian shadow theater and puppet theater have long, honored histories. Iranians are still building on these traditions. New puppet operas, such as *Rostam and Sohrab*, have brought large audiences to the Ferdowsi Hall in Tehran.

Movies

Iranian filmmakers have been producing quality cinema since the early 1900s. The most common films today are serious dramas and action films. The dramas focus on hardships of everyday life, although writers are usually careful not to directly criticize either the government or Islam. All films are censored, and one that is too critical might never be shown.

Many Iranian films are screened in the West. Saman Salour's *Sizdah 59* explores the challenges that Iranian war veterans face in their daily lives. *Lonely Tune of Tehran*, an earlier film by Salour, was shown at the prestigious Cannes Film Festival in France.

Just as in Hollywood, Iran has its share of filmmaking families. The best known is the Makhmalbaf family. Mohsen Makhmalbaf writes, directs, edits, and produces his own films. His 2001 film *Kandahar* was selected by *Time* magazine as one of the top one hundred films of all time. His wife, Marzieh Meshkini, has earned thirteen international prizes for her films. The most popular was *The Day I Became a Woman*, about her life as a woman in Iran. Daughters Samira and Hana have both directed films. Makhmalbaf is also known as a humanitarian for his work helping children from war-torn Afghanistan go to Iran to get an education.

Mohsen Makhmalbaf has directed more than twenty films.

Iranian folk music is often performed in cultural centers throughout the country.

Music

Iranian music and dancing have been part of life's celebrations since ancient times. The goblet-shaped *tombak* and the frame drum, called a *daf*, have pounded out rhythms for centuries, while the high-pitched *ney*, a reed flute, trilled the melodies of songs in praise of beauty and bravery. This is the folk music of Iran. It is still heard over the radio and on recordings.

In the nineteenth and twentieth centuries, classical music, operas, and symphonies filled the halls of major Iranian cities. Musicians studied at a conservatory in Tehran, where composers and conductors were encouraged to experience all forms of music.

In 1979, the new Islamic government closed the conservatory and outlawed some forms of Western music. Rock, hip-hop, and rap, popular with Iranian youth, are illegal. Yet some forms of rock, pop, blues, jazz, and other forms of Western music are still heard. Young people listen to their favorite artists over the Internet and on satellite radio. CDs are popular, and artists perform in concerts, even though there is always a threat of punishment by the government. Iranian musicians such as the pop artist Googoosh have left Iran for the United States or Europe. Some upload their songs onto the Internet and let Iranian youth download them for free.

A Land of Poets

Iran has long been known as a land of poets. Poetry is read, recited, and repeated in homes and classrooms. It is the medium through which Iran's greatest writers have expressed joy, sorrow, loss, and pride. Shahs and other leaders supported court poets. Every court had its poet, and every heroic deed was recorded in epic form.

Iran has several great poets. The most popular include Rumi, Ferdowsi, Hafez, and Sa'di. Jalal ad-Din Muhammad Balkhi, better known as Rumi, wrote in the thirteenth century. His major work is the *Mathnawi*, a collection of twenty-seven

Googoosh

Faegheh Atashin, nicknamed Googoosh, is a native of Tehran. Born in 1950, she began singing publicly at the age of five. At ten, she performed in movies. By the time she was nineteen, Googoosh had become an Iranian pop star. Over the course of twenty-five years, Googoosh appeared in forty films, recorded more than two hundred songs in Persian, and performed in concerts. Immediately after the Islamic Revolution, Googoosh stopped performing. In 2000, she broke her silence and embarked on a world tour. A recent album, *Akharin Khabar,* broke all Persian sales records.

thousand lines of poetry about Sufi Islamic beliefs. In the tenth century, Hakim Abul-Qasim Ferdowsi wrote the *Shahnameh*, an epic poem of Iranian kings and heroes. All Iranian students read the *Shahnameh*. In the story, the hero Rostam is a larger-than-life character who faces major obstacles, battles demons, and always comes out the victor.

Iranian children and adults delight in many of the fairy tales popular in Iran. *One Thousand and One Nights* is the story of Scheherazade, who amuses her husband by telling a story each night for 1,001 nights. Each tale ends in suspense, and the husband has to wait until the following night to hear the next chapter. Folktales remain popular, and Iran's fairy tales feature princes, thieves, and magic.

Iranian readers enjoy detective stories, love stories, and action novels, most of which have happy endings, cruel vil-

Books are sold at vendor stalls as well as traditional bookstores.

Persepolis

In the year 2000, writer and illustrator Marjane Satrapi wrote *Persepolis,* a graphic novel about her youth in Iran during and after the Islamic Revolution. The book consists of black-and-white cartoons, and deals with her leaving and eventually returning to Iran. The book became a best seller. It was made into an animated film and won a prize at the 2007 Cannes Film Festival.

lains, and victorious heroes. The Islamic government controls publishing, and fiction cannot openly violate the government's interpretation of Islamic standards. Many of Iran's most famous authors no longer live in Iran. Shahriar Mandanipour could not get his writing published in Iran and moved to the United States in 2006. His first novel printed in English was *Censoring an Iranian Love Story,* published in 2009. Marjane Satrapi, author of the graphic novel *Persepolis,* currently lives in Paris.

In the Arena

Iran's athletes compete in a number of team and individual sports. Traditional sports include bodybuilding, wrestling, polo, and a traditional Iranian version of gymnastics. Iranians also excel in modern sports such as soccer, basketball, tae kwon do, judo, and weight lifting.

Traditional Iranian gymnastics and bodybuilding took place in the *zurkhaneh,* which means "the house of strength." This is an octagonal pit with seating around the outside for athletes, musicians, and the audience. Athletes strive to achieve great strength through purity and gymnastics, using wooden clubs, metal shields, and iron weights.

Historians believe that polo was introduced in Iran centuries ago. In polo, two teams compete on horseback to knock a ball through a goal. Riding skills, balance, and endurance were useful in battles, and polo was a type of military practice. Although polo lost popularity in the twentieth century, there is some renewed interest in playing it.

Popular Sports

The most popular sport in Iran is soccer. Iranian teams have won the Asian Club Championship, and the Iranian national team has competed in the World Cup three times. While

Women and the Olympics

Iranian women rarely take part in public sports. Because of the dress restrictions Iran imposes, they usually participate in sports within athletic clubs and gyms that cater to girls and women. It would seem almost impossible for a woman to get a place on Iran's Olympic team. But teen markswoman Nassim Hassanpour (right) made it. She was the only female athlete on Iran's 2004 Summer Olympics team. She was able to enter the 10-meter air pistol event because the activity enabled her to wear the headscarf and body covering required by her government. Since the Islamic Revolution, only six women athletes have represented Iran in the Olympics. Three female athletes competed in shooting, and one each competed in archery, rowing, and tae kwon do.

Hossein Rezazadeh

Called the Iranian Hercules, Hossein Rezazadeh (1978–) is an Olympic gold-medal winning weight lifter. He competed in the super heavyweight class and was the first Iranian to win two gold medals. In 2002, Rezazadeh was voted the Champion of Champions of Iran.

less popular, Iran's weight lifters, wrestlers, and martial artists compete successfully in international competitions.

Women compete in soccer, but they must wear headscarves and uniforms that cover their arms, legs, and hair. Iran's national women's team hoped to compete in the 2012 Olympics in London, but FIFA, the world soccer organization, prohibits displays of political, religious, or commercial interests on uniforms. FIFA declared that wearing headscarves is a religious symbol, and the women's team could not compete. Islamic laws do not allow the women to compete without their heads covered.

Iran has professional leagues for both basketball and volleyball. Iran sends teams to the Olympics, and its national basketball team won a gold medal in the 2007 FIBA Asia Championship. Hamed Haddadi plays center for the Memphis Grizzlies, making him the first Iranian to play professional basketball in the United States. Volleyball is extremely popular, and Iran's national youth and junior teams have won medals in the Under-19 and Under-21 World Championships. In 2007, the Under-19 team won a gold medal in the world championship in Mexico.

Family and Community

ZAHRA AND SAEED ARE MODERN YOUNG IRANIANS.
They met when Saeed came to buy shoes at Zahra's family
shop in the bazaar. They have seen each other several times
at local parks and have gone hiking in the mountains outside
Tehran. They hope to marry, and Saeed's parents will visit
Zahra's family to formally ask her consent to wed.

Opposite: **In Iran, life revolves around family.**

In the rural village of Kalakan, Zelal has reached marriage-
able age. Her family raises sheep and is highly respected in the
village. Her father is on the council of elders. Erez has seen
Zelal in the village, but they have never spoken. Erez's parents
approached Zelal's family about the possibility of a match.
Erez and Zelal will have an arranged marriage. In villages and
among the most traditional families, an arranged marriage is
the customary way a couple gets married.

The Wedding

Iranian weddings have two parts, the *Aghd* and the *Jashn-e
Aroosi*. The Aghd is the legal process of getting married. The
bride, groom, and their witnesses sign the marriage contract.
The witnesses are often male relatives. The Aghd takes place

Weddings are cause for great celebration in Iran.

at the home of the bride's parents. The groom sits on the right and the bride on the left, both facing east. They sit at the head of the *Sofreh Aghd*, the wedding spread.

The Sofreh Aghd is an arrangement of symbolic items that are laid out on luxurious fabric. A full-size mirror represents fate, and two candelabras signify the brightness of the future for the bride and groom. On a tray lay seven spices, including poppy seeds, wild rice, angelica, salt, nigella seeds, black tea, and frankincense. These herbs and spices guard the lives of the couple and protect them against witchcraft. The spread features a flat bread called *noon-e sangak*, which represents wealth. Decorated eggs, almonds, and walnuts in their shells symbolize fertility, or the ability to have children. Pomegranates and apples stand for a happy future. Rose water freshens the air, while *espand*, a type of incense, ensures good health. A bowl made from crystallized sugar rounds out the display to sweeten the lives of the married couple.

The bride wears a white dress, much like brides wear in North America or Europe. The groom wears a dark suit or tuxedo. Traditionally, the groom is asked if he takes his bride in marriage, and he answers immediately. The bride is then asked, and she does not answer until she has been asked three times. The bride and groom sit under a cloth held by close relatives. Sugar cubes are rubbed above their heads to represent sweetness and joy in marriage.

The Jashn-e Aroosi is the wedding reception, which includes several days of feasting and celebrating. Guests will see beautiful flowers, plenty of fresh fruit and delicious foods, and vast amounts of jewelry. A buffet-style dinner nearly always features *javaher polow*, a rice dish with bits of orange

Iranian wedding receptions often feature music and dancing.

Learning from Last Names

In Iran, many last names have endings that indicate something about the person or the person's family. Family names have only been in use since 1919. Before that, people were known by a string of titles that may have led to confusion about a person's identity. Using a last name was required by law after 1919.

Ending	Meaning	Example
-nejad or -nezad	Descendant of	Mahmoud Ahmadinejad
-i	From or of a place	Ruhollah Khomeini
-pur, -pour, -zad, -zadeh	Son of or child of	Christiane Amanpour
-doust	Friend	Hossein Fardoust
-ian	Of or related to	Ali Nassirian

peel, almonds, sugar, berries, and pistachios. Gold and gem-stone-covered jewelry are typical gifts for a bride. Her wedding gifts remain her personal property, even if the couple divorces. They are the wife's wealth.

The Aroosi traditionally lasted three to seven days. Modern weddings try to limit the Aroosi, although even the reduced version can be quite lavish.

The Family

The core of Iranian and Islamic life is the family. In Iran, family, kinship, and community are essential to the happiness of all people. Family is more important than friends or business relationships. When a couple marries, the bride usually keeps her family name and does not use her husband's name. Children born to the couple bear their father's last name.

Historically, women could marry at puberty, which meant girls as young as eight or nine were sometimes married. Boys married between ages twelve and fifteen. By 2000, the legal

age for girls to marry was raised to thirteen. Most people wait to marry until they are in their twenties. Today, the average age for an Iranian woman to marry is twenty-two. Men are usually about twenty-six.

The average Iranian family has two children.

The birth of a child is important for a young couple. In Muslim families, when a baby is born, a family elder will whisper a Muslim prayer into the baby's ears. The baby will hear those same words calling the faithful to prayer at a mosque. Grandmothers help take care of mother and baby for at least ten days.

Parents choose the baby's name, although close relatives may offer suggestions. Boys are given names that indicate strength, power, or courage. The most common boys' names are Muhammad, Ali, Hossein, and Mahdi. Girls are given

Family and Community **119**

According to Iranian death customs, close relatives of the deceased dress in black, often for forty days.

names that refer to beauty, gentleness, or joy. Popular girls' names include Fatemeh, Zahra, Sara, Zeinab, and Maryam.

A Typical Funeral

According to Iranian custom, a person should be buried quickly, within twenty-four hours of death. The body should be washed and wrapped in a white burial shroud. The person who does the washing must be a Muslim and the same sex as the deceased. Several attempts are made to put the body into a coffin, succeeding on the fourth try. This is to represent the refusal of the dead to leave their earthly lives behind. Verses from the Qur'an are recited, and relatives dress in black. The family provides a feast as a memorial to the deceased's life and contributions to the family and the Iranian culture.

Islam and Daily Life

Islam, like most religions, is a way of life. Although citizens are allowed to practice the religion to whatever degree they want, in public they must follow the laws set down by the Islamic government.

Teens live very differently in Iran than in the United States. Boys may wear jeans and T-shirts but not in a mosque or school. Girls wear clothing much like clothes worn in North America. However, laws require that girls wear conservative dress in public, which means at least a headscarf and a *manto*, which resembles a long, thin trench coat. Boys and girls are separated in schools, and children wear school uniforms.

Western-style clothing is available at many shops in cities such as Tehran.

The government forbids boys and girls from partying and dancing together, but many Iranians ignore these restrictions. Teens listen to music in their homes or over the Internet. Since dating is prohibited, young Iranians log on to the Internet to chat and arrange meetings.

Women must cover their heads in public. The traditional head cover, called a *hijab*, hides a woman's hair. Women who choose to dress in more Western styles of clothing must cover their hair and arms, and wear longer skirts in public. When in public, some women keep their face mostly covered.

Iranian women can drive, vote, and own property, but they are not granted automatic divorces as their husbands are. They have to show cause for the court to grant them a divorce. If a couple gets divorced, it is the husband's choice, and he usually gets custody of the children. Women can hold public office,

Iranian women pursue a wide variety of careers.

and many women have served in the Majles and the executive branch of government, but not at the highest levels.

Iranian families typically share meals together.

In the Home

The dinner table in most Iranian homes is a feast for the taste buds and the eyes. Iranian dishes often mix meats or poultry with fruits, nuts, and spices. The ideal meal is a delicious blend of sweet, sour, salty, and spicy flavors. Duck with berries and pistachio nuts, or lamb with onions, prunes, and cumin are served with bread or rice. The most popular meat is lamb, which is raised in most regions of Iran. Chicken, fish, and duck are found in most markets, but beef is expensive, so it is not often served for a family meal. Iranians never eat pork because Islam forbids it. A family favorite is kebabs—meat or fish on skewers—grilled over hot coals and served with rice or bread.

Salad Shirazi

Iranians eat salads with many meals. In this recipe, a cucumber and tomato salad is spiced up with some mint.

Ingredients

2 cucumbers

4 medium tomatoes

8 ounces fresh mint

4 tablespoons fresh lime juice

1 medium onion

3 tablespoons olive oil

½ teaspoon salt

¼ teaspoon pepper

Directions

1. Wash and peel the cucumbers. Wash the tomatoes and mint. Peel the onion.
2. Chop the cucumbers into small cubes, about ¼ inch on a side. Chop the tomatoes and onions into small cubes. Mix in a medium-size bowl.
3. Chop the mint very finely and add to the vegetables.
4. In a small bowl, mix the lime juice, olive oil, salt, and pepper. Blend well and pour over the vegetables.
5. Mix well, and refrigerate for at least one hour before serving.

Iranians eat a variety of fruits, including dates, raisins, melons, pomegranates, plums, apricots, and peaches. When in season, fruits are eaten fresh. During winter months, dried plums, peaches, and apricots are used in cooking. Vegetables such as carrots, potatoes, and onions are added to stews. Salad vegetables, particularly tomatoes and cucumbers, are served regularly.

Rice and fresh bread are served with most dinners. Stews and casseroles are served over rice, which may be mixed with currants, pistachios, and onions. Flat breads are served warm with most meals.

Breakfast, called *sobhaaneh*, is usually sweet Persian tea, flat bread, butter or cheese, and jam. Eggs are also common. The tea is chai, which is hot and sweet. In some areas, breakfast is a wheat cereal, called *haleem*, which may contain shredded lamb or turkey.

Lunch and dinner in Iran are similar. Both are cooked meals, both include rice and bread, and both have mixtures of meat, vegetables, dairy, and fruit.

For a quick meal, Iranians turn to fast foods. Kebab shops are found in most cities, but Western-style fast foods have long been common, especially in Tehran, Mashhad, and other large cities. Pizza, hamburgers, hot dogs, deli sandwiches, and fried chicken have been popular for decades, but they are often prepared Iranian-style and do not always taste like the American versions. Chinese and Japanese restaurants, while not common, draw big crowds in Tehran, along with Italian restaurants, where lasagna is a hit. Sodas, fruit juices, fruit smoothies, or *dooghs* (yogurt, mint, soda water, and ice) are refreshing drinks.

Iranians sometimes hold Norooz celebrations outdoors.

Celebrating Together

In addition to religious holidays, Iranians celebrate a handful of national holidays that honor major events in their history. On these days, schools, banks, and most businesses are closed.

Norooz, or New Year, is the year's biggest celebration. Norooz is March 21, and a short holiday usually follows. The celebration of Norooz dates back to the Zoroastrian celebration of the beginning of spring, when the sun began to strengthen, days lengthened, and flowers bloomed.

Iranians prepare for Norooz by giving their homes a good cleaning. Traditionally, this was the time to buy new shoes. Today, Iranians celebrate by buying new outfits. Families and friends get together, sharing meals or meeting in public gardens.

It is important to set up a Norooz table in the home. On this table are items that all begin with the letter *s* in Persian. *Seeb* (an apple) stands for beauty, and *sabzeh* (wheat sprouts) represents the rebirth that comes with spring. *Sumac* (spice) is for new life, while *senjed* (lotus fruit) is for love. *Serkeh* (vinegar) stands for patience, *samanu* (wheat germ paste) represents wealth, and *sir* (garlic) is for good health. This custom comes from the Zoroastrian celebration that welcomed spring. A good start at Norooz will bring a good year for the entire family.

Sizdah Be-dar is held on the last or thirteenth day of Norooz. This day represents a return to everyday life—including school and work—after twelve days of Norooz. On Sizdah Be-dar, city families pack picnic lunches and head to the countryside or to local parks and gardens. During Norooz, families plant a container of wheat or barley, which sprouts during the thirteen-day New Year celebration. On Sizdah Be-dar, the custom is to throw away the sprouts, which gets rid of sickness, pain, and bad luck. Once this is done, Iranian families get back to the realities of daily life.

Timeline

Iranian History

Tehran becomes the capital.	**1795**
Nasser al-Din Shah sells mining, banking, and railroad opportunities to Great Britain.	**1800s**
Following the Constitutional Revolution, the Majles, the first lawmaking body in Iran, is formed.	**1906**
Reza Shah seizes power.	**1925**
British and Russian troops oust Reza Shah and replace him with Mohammad Reza Shah.	**1941**
Ayatollah Khomeini is jailed for rebelling against the shah.	**1963**
The Islamic Revolution ends the shah's rule; Khomeini becomes the supreme leader.	**1979**
The Iran-Iraq War begins.	**1980**
The Iran-Iraq War ends.	**1988**
Khomeini dies; Khamenei is named supreme leader.	**1989**
Shirin Ebadi becomes Iran's first winner of the Nobel Peace Prize.	**2003**

World History

1865	The American Civil War ends.
1879	The first practical lightbulb is invented.
1914	World War I begins.
1917	The Bolshevik Revolution brings communism to Russia.
1929	A worldwide economic depression begins.
1939	World War II begins.
1945	World War II ends.
1957	The Vietnam War begins.
1969	Humans land on the Moon.
1975	The Vietnam War ends.
1989	The Berlin Wall is torn down as communism crumbles in Eastern Europe.
1991	The Soviet Union breaks into separate states.
2001	Terrorists attack the World Trade Center in New York City and the Pentagon near Washington, D.C.
2004	A tsunami in the Indian Ocean destroys coastlines in Africa, India, and Southeast Asia.
2008	The United States elects its first African American president.

Fast Facts

Official name: Islamic Republic of Iran

Capital: Tehran

Official language: Persian

Tehran

Iranian flag

Mount Damavand

Official religion:	Shi'i Islam
National anthem:	*"Soroud-e Melli-e Jomhouri-e Eslami-e Iran"* ("Anthem of the Islamic Republic of Iran")
Type of government:	Islamic republic
Chief of state:	Supreme leader
Head of government:	President
Area:	636,296 square miles (1,648,000 sq km)
Latitude and longitude of geographic center:	32°N, 53° E
Bordering countries:	Iraq and Turkey to the west; Armenia and Azerbaijan to the northwest, Turkmenistan to the northeast; Afghanistan and Pakistan to the east
Bordering bodies of water:	Persian Gulf and Gulf of Oman to the south; Caspian Sea to the north
Highest elevation:	Mount Damavand, 18,806 feet (5,732 m) above sea level
Lowest elevation:	Caspian Sea, 92 feet (28 m) below sea level
Average January temperatures (Tehran):	High: 46.2°F (7.9°C); low: 30°F (−1°C)
Average July temperatures (Tehran):	High: 97.9°F (36.6°C); low: 79°F (26°C)

Shiraz

Lowest recorded temperature:	Saqqez, −32.8°F (−36°C)
Highest recorded temperature:	Dasht-e Lut Desert, 159°F (71°C)
National population:	76,923,300 (2010 est.)

Population of major cities (2010 est.):

Tehran	8,429,807
Mashhad	2,965,000
Shiraz	1,750,000
Tabriz	1,698,000
Isfahan	1,630,000

Landmarks:

▶ *Azadi Tower,* Tehran

▶ *Blue Mosque,* Tabriz

▶ *Grand Bazaar,* Tehran

▶ *Persepolis*

Economy: Petroleum products (crude oil and natural gas) are Iran's major industries. The country manufactures automobiles, iron and steel products, and textiles. Iran also processes food, mainly refining sugar and vegetable oils. Major agricultural products in Iran include wheat, barley, rice, sugar beets, and sugarcane. The nation is among global leaders in producing raisins and pistachio nuts.

Currency: Rial. In 2011, 10,578 rials equaled US$1.

System of weights and measures: Metric system

Literacy rate: 77%

Currency

Student

Omar Khayyám

Common Persian words and phrases:

salaam	hello
khodaa-haafez	good-bye
khaahesh meekenam	please
mersee	thank you
baleh	yes
nakheyr	no
ma'zerat meekhaaham	excuse me
sobh-bekheyr	good morning
Hal-e shoman chetoreh?	How are you?
khoobam, mersee	fine, thank you

Famous Iranians:

Mahmoud Ahmadinejad (1956–)
President

Shirin Ebadi (1947–)
Winner of the Nobel Peace Prize

Googoosh (1950–)
Pop singer

Ayatollah Sayyed Ali Khamenei (1939–)
Supreme leader

Omar Khayyám (ca. 1048–ca. 1132 CE)
Poet

Ayatollah Ruhollah Khomeini (1902–1989)
Islamic Republic founder

Mohsen Makhmalbaf (1957–)
Filmmaker

To Find Out More

Books

▶ Bardhan-Quallen, Sudipta. *Iran.* Farmington Hills, MI: Blackbirch Press, 2005.

▶ Broyles, Matthew. *Mahmoud Ahmadinejad: President of Iran.* New York: Rosen Publishing, 2008.

▶ Crompton, Samuel Willard. *Cyrus the Great.* New York: Chelsea House, 2008.

▶ Downing, David. *Iran.* Tarrytown, NY: Marshall Cavendish Benchmark, 2008.

▶ Graham, Amy. *Iran in the News: Past, Present, and Future.* Berkeley Heights, NJ: MyReportLinks.com Books, 2006.

▶ Murphy, John. *Ali Khamenei.* New York: Chelsea House, 2008.

▶ Satrapi, Marjane. *Persepolis.* New York: Pantheon Books, 2003.

▶ Schomp, Virginia. *The Ancient Persians.* Tarrytown, NY: Marshall Cavendish Benchmark, 2010.

▶ Seidman, David. *Teens in Iran.* Minneapolis: Compass Point Books, 2008.

Music

▶ *Raghshaye Irani.* Caltex Records, 2006. Sound recording.

▶ *The Rough Guide to the Music of Iran.* World Music Network, 2006. Sound recording.

Web Sites

▶ **BBC News—Iran Country Profile**
http://news.bbc.co.uk/2/hi/middle_east/country_profiles/790877.stm
Find out more about Iran from the BBC.

▶ **A Celebration of Women Writers: Writers from Iran**
http://digital.library.upenn.edu/women/_generate/IRAN.html
Read the works of Iran's women writers at the Web site of the University of Pennsylvania's digital library.

▶ **Persian Carpet**
www.persian-carpet.info
An old and honored craft, Persian rugs are prized throughout the world. Learn about the history of these beautiful, handwoven masterpieces.

▶ **Tehran**
http://tehran.stanford.edu/imagemap/tehran.html
Find out more about Tehran, a modern urban center in an ancient land.

Embassy

▶ **Representative of the Office of Iran**
c/o Embassy of Pakistan
2209 Wisconsin Avenue NW
Washington, DC 20007

▶ **Visit this Scholastic Web site for more information on Iran:**
www.factsfornow.scholastic.com

Index

Page numbers in *italics* indicate illustrations.

Meet the Author

BARBARA SOMERVILL HAS BEEN A WRITER FOR MANY years. She loves learning about new places, cultures, and cuisines. Learning about Iran for this book was fascinating. One thing that always interests her is how people live their daily lives. Somervill could not go directly to Iran to find out this information, but she did get to visit via YouTube. Someday, Somervill hopes to visit Iran, but, in the meantime, YouTube, books, and DVDs provide armchair travel experience.

Photo Credits